Essay Index

A MUSICIAN AT LARGE
BY HARVEY GRACE

'Serioso, ma non troppo,
Commodetto, non pomposo,
Leggiero, e scherzoso,
Intimamentissimo . . .

Essay Index Reprint Series

Essay Index

originally published by

OXFORD UNIVERSITY PRESS

BOOKS FOR LIBRARIES PRESS
FREEPORT, NEW YORK

First Published 1928
Reprinted 1970

STANDARD BOOK NUMBER:
8369-1506-2

LIBRARY OF CONGRESS CATALOG CARD NUMBER:
78-107703

PRINTED IN THE UNITED STATES OF AMERICA

To

PREFACE

THIS collection of articles from the *Musical Times* is made (incredible as it may appear) on the suggestion of several readers. I am indebted to the Editor of that journal for his ready permission to reprint.

A volume of this kind resembles an anthology, in that every reader will disapprove of certain choices. Author and anthologist alike, however, cheer themselves with the reflection that, as no two readers will agree as to what should have been omitted, the selection as a whole may justify itself.

The articles have been carefully revised, a good deal of fresh material added, and much that has proved to be of merely passing interest removed.

In certain chapters of a controversial nature I have, for the sake of both fairness and clearness, retained the *ipsissima verba* of the critics who took part in the original discussion. Having left their words, I felt bound also to leave their names. I hope they won't mind.

On the other hand, if the blunt criticism and personal references in the chapter on 'Brows, High and Low,' give offence, I shall feel no compunction. They are reprinted—as they were written—deliberately, because I feel strongly that we musicians have given the perpetrators of bad music too long an innings. We have allowed the public judgement to go

by default, whereas we should have stirred ourselves
to expose the pretensions of so-called 'popular' composers. Nor should their apostles escape, even (or,
rather, especially) when the apostle happens to be what
the small child called 'an epistle'—and a viscountess
as well.

CHISLEHURST,
February 1928.

CONTENTS

Guides to the Opera 1

Shakespeare's Use of Music . . . 15

Humour in Music 27

Four-handed Adventures 35

Musical Journalism a Hundred Years ago . 46

Hearing with the Eye 59

Short Cuts and Royal Roads . . . 71

Robbery with Violence 83

Kings and Queens, Assorted . . . 91

Beethoven: Portraits and Perversions . . 97

Beethoven's Mental Powers . . . 104

Beethoven as a Letter-Writer . . . 112

Brows, High and Low 125

Art—Aristocratic or Popular? . . . 139

Jingle at the Ballet 149

On Paper 154

Spirit or Letter? 165

Our Exclusives 173

Cliché and Commonplace 180

Why not Plain English? 196

Actions and Reactions 203

Music and Tears 212

A Defence of Opera 224

Musical Criticism 235

GUIDES TO THE OPERA

ON my shelves stands a whole row of them, of all shapes and sizes, from Kobbé's *Complete Opera Book* of nearly a thousand pages down to the neat little pocket guides of Corbett-Smith, and hardly anywhere can be found more desolating narrative styles. The average opera story is too often a poor thing; why need it be further enfeebled by the baldness of its setting forth in these opera guide books? Krehbiel did his best to make it something better than a dreary catalogue of facts. Here is a passage almost at random from *Pagliacci*:

> Hark to the bagpipes! Huzza [did anybody ever say 'huzza!' except on paper?], here come the *zampognari!* Drone pipes droning and chaunters skirling—as well as they can skirl in Italian! Now we have people and pipers on the stage and there's a bell in the steeple ringing for vespers. Therefore a chorus. Not that we have anything to say that concerns the story in any way. 'Din, don!' That would suffice, but if you must have more: 'Let's to church. Din, don. All's right with love and the sunset. Din, don.'

But this method of agreeably rattling soon palls, and does not solve the difficulty of telling an opera story briefly and in such a way that it becomes good fiction.

Kobbé is content to give us the facts, and, above all, he remains serious. Here is his version of this same scene:

> Just then the bagpipers from a neighbouring village are heard approaching. The musicians, followed by the people of their village, arrive to join in their festival. All are made welcome, and the villagers, save a few who are waiting for Canio and Beppe, go off down the road towards the village. The villagers sing the pretty chorus 'Din, don—suona vespero' ('Ding, dong—the

vespers bell'). Canio nods good-bye to Nedda. He
and Beppe go towards the village. Nedda is alone.
Canio's words and manner worry her.

And thus Kobbé goes his way with no frills, and with
the customary and wearying insistence on the present
tense.

Corbett-Smith is a trifle too anxious to make the
yarns interesting: there is a touch of desperation in
his sprightliness. It reminds me of the extraordinary
delusions that seized some of the Press early in the
post-war period—that London needed 'brightening',
and that the way to 'brighten' her was for folk to
dance and play rag-time till three in the morning,
and have music-hall entertainments in hotels at midnight. Moreover, we were exhorted to smile as we
walked the streets. Apparently this ghastly idea
spread even to the usually sensible provinces, for I
read in the paper that at some school in the country
a prize had been put up for the boy who smiled most
persistently, the winner being a youth who, we were
told, had a smile that had not come off once during
the competitive period. His portrait was given—with
smile—a portrait that made one long to be behind him,
armed with something flat, flexible, and fitting, catching him bending, in order to give the durability of
his grin a really searching test.

Corbett-Smith as operatic story-teller is a little bit
like that youngster. I take up at random one of his
little books—that dealing with *The Magic Flute*—and
open it speculatively, to find him first telling us how
the opera came to be written. Schikaneder and
Mozart are discussing the matter:

But then there came a serious hitch with *The Magic
Flute*. Schikaneder discovered, to his consternation,
that another opera upon the same story had been produced with great success at a rival theatre. Your
theatrical manager, however, must never be at a loss,
and Schikaneder, as I have said, knew his business.

2

'We have got to alter all this, my dear Wolfgang,' he remarked, 'so the sooner we start the better.'

So they talked it over.

'Now let me see,' said Schikaneder. 'That first Act must stay as it is; it is a good opening, and any way it is a far better bit of stage-work than old Muller's version. But after that? We've got to strike out a new line. Something really up-to-date. What can we put in? . . . Well, how about a drink?' (I am quite sure a bottle of wine appeared at that juncture.)

'By Jove!' Schikaneder exclaimed, 'I've got it! Free-masonry! The very thing. The topic of the moment.'

Et cetera, sempre molto scherzoso.

And, in telling the story:

. . . the Queen of Night is a young woman who is evidently incapable of educating her daughter properly, and that is why Sarastro took Pamina away—an inspector of the Board of Education, I imagine, and another 'intelligent anticipation' on the part of Schika-neder.

No; I don't feel that Corbett-Smith has found the way out, though he should receive credit for having produced a capital and convenient series of booklets.

There is something to be said for the curt, business-like method of J. Walker McSpadden in his *Opera Synopses*. McSpadden wastes no words, and gives us the whole of a complicated plot while Krehbiel and Corbett-Smith are merely getting their coats off and spitting on their hands, so to speak. Here, for example, is Act v, of *Manon*, complete in about fifty words:

ACT v.—The Open Road near Havre. Manon is being escorted out of the country by a guard of soldiers. The chevalier asks Lescaut, her cousin, to aid him in rescuing her. They try bribery. She has a short inter-view with Des Grieux, begging his pardon for wreck-ing his life; then perishes from excitement and over-fatigue.

The only satisfactory alternative to this bovrilized method is one in which at least some of the conversation of the characters is reproduced in good, well-written dialogue. Opera tales make such flat reading because of the almost entire absence of conversation. In a well-told story the characters are differentiated and developed by means of dialogue; without it they are mere dummies. I once knew a boy who chose his fiction by the rough-and-ready method of twirling the pages over. If they were full of solid print the book was not for him. 'No conversation,' he would say succinctly. He liked to see the pages with lots of space and irregular columns. His mates used to make fun of his method of choice, but I have since come to the conclusion that he was a better critic than he knew. The best stories are usually those in which the characters speak for themselves, give the atmosphere, develop the plot, and in so doing reveal their own individuality. The writer who gives us little more than incidents and description is a reporter, and most opera guides are dull because they are merely a string of feebly written reports.

§

The one operatic guide to which I can and do come back with enjoyment is the worst of the lot—*The New Opera Glass*, by Fr. (Fritz?) Charley, published at Leipzig about 1895.

I do not bring it forward as a great discovery. A copy has been on my shelves for a dozen years, and a fair number of people are similarly blessed. But the number is small enough to justify my making a few extracts.

The Preface tells us that the book was designed for the benefit of English and American visitors to the Continent; that it found a good—though probably disrespectful—market is shown by its having in 1900 reached a fourth edition. The odd thing is that Charley should have complacently allowed his 'howlers' to remain. He says in his note to the fourth edition that it has been

   . . . revised and augmented from the author through nearly thirdy new operas,

and hopes it

   . . . may find the same kindly reception which has been proved to the fare-gone editions.

It may have been augmented from the author through thirdy new operas, but the revision was very casual. Yet, oddly enough, some of the synopses are written in good English. How came it that the writer of these allowed the remainder to appear in one of the funniest travesties of our language that can be met with? One suspects a touch of malice on the part of the colleague. Or perhaps Charley fancied himself as a linguist, and was above asking for help. How much he needed somebody at his elbow is shown by the result of his wrestlings with the story of *Turandot*:

Turandot.

Kalaf, prince of Assam has leaved his fatherland; after the death of his father, a relates has takes possess of the throne. He intended to enter in service of the prince of Kaschmir. Coming to the castel, he is recognised from the gardener, but he do'nt like to be known him. He has saved the prince his life justly, but is gone away not awaiting the thanks.

Both leaves the stage.

Now Turandot, daughter of the prince of Kaschmir, is carry on the stage; also the parrot is brought, which Kalaf had catched. Turandot and Kalaf falling in love together. Kalaf does choose a favor; he beggs to can loose the riddle Turandot. All are astonished, Turandot herselves, who may save the live of the stranger; but Kalaf remains on his desire.

Second Act: Turandot is happy: Kalaf has loosed all her riddle and she hopes now to get him als bridegroom but Kalaf gives non himself such a riddle, which had to loose Turandot, to tell him his name and his native. But she is sorry, she can not find out the right name and so she is loosing all hopes; all troubles are vainless. Till, at last, she heard the name: Achmed of Samarkand. But this is not the right name: Great meeting. Turandot is greeting as Prince Achmed of Samarkand, but must hear from him, that this is not the right name. In a humble manner she say, that Kalaf must be her Master and commander and that a hearth that deeply loves, much better is, than humour and mind.

Turandot and Kalaf have found to another and enjoyment is everywhere.

Especially among the readers.

We meet with this confusion between 'hearts' and 'hearths' elsewhere—e. g. in Charley's version of Act II of *Romeo and Juliet*:

Second Act: Pavillon in Capulets garden. Romeo singing from the love to Julia; Julia going in the garden, singing also from the love to Romeo. Their hearths are finding together and after lovely sweers are going from another.

'Lovely sweers' for the young couple's vows is one of Charley's happiest feats, though he remains at a good level in his description of the final catastrophe:

Fifth Act: Romeo enter; he is seeing his wife Julia in the apparent death. In the meaning of her really death he is thrinking a bottle poison wishing to be united with her also in the death. In the same moment Julia awaked. Willing to fly the death is coming: Romeo falling on the bottom, Julia takes the sword and murdered herselves.

Even Shakespeare's titles do not escape improvement. Taubert's *Cesario* is said to be 'after Shakespeare's wonderfull piece *What you like*, well known in the whole world'. *The Taming of the Shrew* appears in the body of the book as *The Taming of the Refractory*, in the Preface as *The Tamings of the Shrew*, and

6

in the index as *Taming of the Refractor*. In the synopsis of Act IV of this play we once more meet with lovers' hearths finding together:

Room in Petruchio's house. Petruchio bursting for anger about all things; nothing can satisfying him. Katharina is nearly broken in the hearth; but she loves him and her refractory ist justly going away. Petruchio also loves her and after some quarrels their hearths are finding together to a happy life.

Charley's version of *The Merry Wives of Windsor* is one of his best efforts. I give it in full, prefacing it with the biographical note about Nicolai:

Otto Nicolai

B. Juny 9th 1810 at Königsberg. Left the house of his most strongly father and take lessons on music by Klein and Zelter. 1833 he accepted a position as organist on the Chancellery at Rome and gained as composer of operas a well known name in the whole Italy. D. May 11th 1849 at Berlin, 8 weeks later as his opera: The merry wifes of Windsor were given at first.

'Juny' leaves us in a state of suspense as to whether June or July is meant. Reference to Grove shows that when Charley says Juny he means June. 'Left the house' is a euphemism for 'ran away'. Nicolai's home, we know, was unhappy, probably because of that most strongly father. In the synopsis, Mistresses Ford and Page and Master Slender appear odd, Teutonized as Mrs. Fluth and Mrs. Reich and Mr. Spärlich.

The merry wifes of Windsor.

Text after Shakespeare.

Sir John has written two love-letters to Mrs. Fluth and Mrs. Reich. They resolved to take reveange to him. After leaving the stage their husband appears attended by Messrs. Spärlich und Cajus. The Stage is changed: Mrs. Fluth awaits Mr. Falstaff. Mrs. Reich entered too and now the wonderfull seene: Mr. Falstaff in the clothes-backets.

7

Second Act: The same play: Falstaff appears at the second time. Now he is putted in the cloths of an old aunt, whom is forbidden the house of Mr. Reich. After some merrily scenes he leaves the house as an old woman, attended by the strike of Mr. Reich's stick.

Third Act: Room in Reich's house. The married couples are in the best humour, the wifes have confessed and now they have the intention the old Falstaff to punish the third time.

Changement of the stage: Midnight, in the forest with a hunting house; all persons appears; at least Falstaff too. The two wifes are greeting him; singing a Terzett. Suddenly ghosts are appearing, amusing herselves to strike Falstaff in the best manner. Cajus and Spärlich the lovers from Anna are also at present; but Anna loves Mr. Fenton, with whom she is band at last for ever.

Of all the merrily scenes, give me that wherein the ghosts are amusing herselves to strike Falstaff in the best manner.

§

I should be failing in my duty if I did not bring to the notice of my readers new or unfamiliar works. Flotow's *Indra* is so neglected that its very title is unknown to most musicians. Let Charley, therefore, tell us all about the plot:

Indra.

In the first act: Jozé, a landlord, is waiting up in the house; chorus of sailors are singing; he tells, that he has leave his quarrelsome wife; but he heard, that she also has leaved her home. Now Indra, slave of Kudru, appears: singing. Pedro, on officer, is fallen in love to the girl, wishing to possess her. Her Lady, Kudru, accepting that. Indra singing now: 'If the night', which has Jozé teached her, a song from on old poor soldier: Camoens, residing under the hearers. Indra is falling in love to Camoens and Pedro, the lover from her, ordered Camoens to his service. Zigaretta, the wife of Jozé is appearing; seeing her husband and soonly she is again the mistress in Jozé's house. . . .

Second act: Port at Lissabon. A church on the one side, and Jozés public house on the other. Camoens teaching Indra to pray; Jozé appears, telling the arrive of a ship from Africa. . . . In a short time after that a canoe with two gentlemen appears; the king and Fernand, the first wounded. The king is recovered by Indra. Pedro discovered Indra and wishing to possess her now. She is renouncing. He declare her as sorceress. Through the king, presented by Camera, silent every where.

Third act: Room in Jozés house; nobody is there; he is mourning; the people avoids his house; wish back again his wife. Sailors appears; beetween their his wife; the first are going away; only his wife stopped; perceiving another and pardoning. Sebastian appears and wish to know the name of the poet from 'the Luciade'. Indra refuse, begging grace for Camoens. But the king is fallen in love to her, wishing to make her to his wife. Pedro, trying the deserter, appears, to get him for the dead. Pedro warning the king: the girl, Indra, beeing heathen. The king himself asked her; hearing the name of Camoens, the famish poet, bending his royal head and giving him Indra to his wife.

So now we know all about *Indra*, though as a matter of detail I don't understand what is meant by Camoens residing under the hearers. Still, it is clear that he was poor, as all poets ought to be, and this makes the expression 'famish poet' singularly neat and appropriate. Nevertheless, I think we may take it that Charley is really thinking of the poet's fame rather than of his *faim*. I am strengthened in this view by the fact that Boïto is alluded to in a biographical note as a 'famish poet'.

This is not the only example of a slip leading to the coining of a happy expression. In the synopsis of *Othello*, Act III, we read:

Receiving the orders from the Dogen of Venedig through a assembly, Othello orders also his wife on

9

the place, but he is wrathful with his wife, warping her on the ground, so that the people is thinking that Othello is fallen suddenly in insanity.

There is a fine summary vigour about this method of putting people out of action by warping them on the ground, and I commend it to those of you who have not yet left off beating your wives. Charley evidently knew he had hit on a good word, for he uses it elsewhere, telling us in *Esmeralda* that

Quasimodo looking out for that [Frollo's rageful rushing on Phœbus] and observing Frollo, is warping himself between the both and is now stabbed instead Phöbus.

That'll learn him to warp. Still, it was not in vain, for

Phöbus and Esmeralda embracing another are happily.

Space is running out, so I must be content with a few of the briefest of extracts. Here is a cryptic passage from *Medea*:

. . . the heart of Dirce is filled with afflicton by remembering on Kolchis, the leaved wife of Jason. But he submit her, beeing allways infortunatly for me.

If you can understand this, you are one up.

Medea was clearly not at all a nice person. We read:

Kreon reprimand her from the Land and is going away passionately. Medea is forced to ge but not before swear bloody vengeance . . . to kill their own children and after them Dirce.

She doesn't bring off the whole coup, for the children are saved:

. . . but Dirce, is dying through her own cloth and diadem, who were filled with poison by Medea.

Medea herself,

. . . with a dagger in the hand, leaves the place, flying through the air upon a wagon volcanic.

'Wagon volcanic' is one of Charley's best.

In *The Barber of Bagdad* he gets confused between 'clocks' and 'cloches':

The clocks call for the prayings. Margiana promised him to be a good daughter, only to receive now Nurreddin. A lovely leisure hour for the both.

Rudely interrupted, however:

The Kadi returns; surprising the lovers: only way: consealing Nurreddin in a box, standing in the room. Nurreddin in the box; the Kadi will open it. . . . Lately the box is opened and Nurreddin leaves his place not quite agreeable. The Kalif, taking interest on this case, ordered the marriage between the lovers. The barber is chained but in the following is pardoned him. With songs on the Kalif, intonated by Abul and the chorus, is closed the interest work.

§

One of my favourite passages is the opening of *Don Pasquale*:

Don Pasquale, an old bachelor, is waiting on Malatesta, his old friend, who tells him, that he has find out a woman for him, beeing his own sister, educated in the cloister, but a nice girl, juste on ange. Pasquale is enthusiasting and begs to becomes acquainting with this lady.

The old rip! But he gets his deserts when a mock marriage ties him for a time to widow Norina, who nags and even boxes his ears. This ear-boxing leads to another new word:

. . . Strong dispute; she is boting him.

'Boting' is perhaps hardly so good as 'warping'; but it has its points as an ingenious blend of beating, boxing, and baiting. All ends happily, you will remember, and Ernesto is duly married to Norina and receives a handsome yearly income—which Charley calls 'granting Ernesto a annually supply'. The happy ending fully justifies the fraud, and so Malatesta was right when he gained Norina

. . . for his plans against Don Pasquale, hoping that all will be good in the farther.

Unwillingly I pass many delicious passages, and take as a final gem the closing sentence of *Cesario* (Taubert's version of *As you like it* or, as Charley calls it, *What you like*):

In the third, latest act, is coming all to a happy end: Sebastian married Oliva, Tobias and Marias, Orsino and Cesareo are becomes happies couppled poirs.

There is something almost delirious in the recklessness of the last four words—a 'howler' of the first water, and one showing Charley led astray once more by his French. His English was not sufficient to show him there are 'pairs' and 'pears'.

Some of the biographical notes are worth a moment's attention. Of Berlioz we read that

. . . his first musical work did not received any succes and he entered the second time at the School of music and was gaining the roman price for one of his 'Cantates'.

We hardly recognize the Prix de Rome under 'roman price'. Berlioz's neglect at home and comparative popularity abroad are thus described:

. . . his compositions were received with a greater applause in the strange as in his own country.

Of Boïto's *Mefistofele* we are told that it

. . . received [1868] a very inferior success, but afterwards, 1875, she gained, after some alteration made by him, a very respectfully success, and now she had made a good way near and far.

§

I close with a glance at the advertisement pages at the end of the book. Here is one calculated to make the reader almost giddy:

Nowhere is to find a shop saling musical instruments who has not bought something from this place.

The undersigned is recommanding his store for every subject in this manner.

The proprietor of the undersigned house, sooner musician, and all his clerks beeing, before musician, can on this reason overtake every garantee for the best execution of all orders.

All persons, ordering something in regards of this annonce are receiving a pretty addition.

Wilhelm Herwig in Markneukirchen, Saxony.

This looks as if Charley not only wrote most of the book but the advertisements as well.

One wonders how such a book reached four editions in about five years. It was of no use to any but readers of English, and its sale was almost entirely confined to English residents and tourists in Germany. As a real guide to the opera it was not very helpful, seeing that Charley so ties himself into knots that some of his versions are not understandable. It seems likely, then, that derisive tourists bought the *New Opera Glass* as a particularly funny example of English as she is wrote, and that the 'kindly reception of the fare-gone editions' which so pleased the author was due to a cause he little suspected. I hear a reader say that Charley's English versions are as good as the German ones most Englishmen could turn out. True; but we English are well aware of our deficiencies as linguists —in fact, we take a foolish pride in them—and I cannot imagine one of us being so venturesome as to write a German book with no better qualifications than a slender vocabulary, a mere hint of grammar, and an abounding confidence in himself and in his German-

13

English dictionary. Anyhow, if there is one so bold he cannot complain if Germans regard his book as a joke.

I return the *New Opera Glass* to its niche among the other guides—Kobbé, Corbett-Smith, Krehbiel, McSpadden, and the rest. When I really want to know something about the opera plots I shall consult them—as I consult a time-table. But when I don't want information—when I want rather a kind of inspired muddle that will amuse and confuse at the same time—I go elsewhere. Kobbé & Co. I merely consult; Charley I read, again and again.

SHAKESPEARE'S USE OF MUSIC

IT is one of the curiosities of Shakespearian criticism
that until recently the musical interpolations, and,
above all, the songs, have never been considered in
their relation to the plays. Even now the subject is
so fresh that many Shakespearian students fail to
grasp its significance. For example, when, in 1916,
Mr. Percy Scholes read before the Musical Association his paper on 'The purpose behind Shakespeare's
use of Music', the subsequent discussion (joined in by
many eminent musicians) had so little relevance that
the lecturer, at the close of the meeting, had to remind
his hearers of the main purport of his paper—Shakespeare's use of music as a vital part of the drama, and
especially in such portions as dealt with the super-
natural, or with such subjects as love, death, madness,
&c. Eight years before Mr. Scholes's paper was read,
Mr. Richmond Noble, of Lincoln College, Oxford, set
to work on a book entitled *Shakespeare's Use of
Songs*; [1] having been goaded thereto by the late
Lewis Waller's transfer of a song from *Love's Labour's
Lost* to *As You Like It*.

Most of us who have attended performances of the
plays have been annoyed again and again by the
ineptitudes of those responsible for the musical side
of the production. The public is ignorant and easy-
going in this matter because musicians themselves
have treated Shakespeare badly.

Composers have set his songs with no more than
a superficial understanding of the text; or they have
used a corrupt text, apparently taking it from antho-
logies or books of recitations instead of going to a good
edition of the plays. Teachers and others who have
the choice of songs in their hands perpetuate some

[1] Oxford University Press.

15

of the least satisfactory settings, merely because these settings happen to be familiar. The matter is one in which no musician has a right to be uninterested or ill-informed, and Mr. Noble's book leaves no excuse for ignorance in the future.

Briefly, his thesis is that the songs in Shakespeare are not pitchforked in for mere variety's sake, but have a definite purpose. Thus they may cover the coming on or going off of a character (Feste's 'I am gone, sir, and anon sir', is a good example of the latter purpose); or express the character of the singer (the misanthropy of Amiens is shown in his two songs, 'Under the greenwood tree' and 'Blow, blow, thou winter wind'); or take the place of scenery in suggesting the locale of the action or the season of the year; or provide cover for by-play, and so on. Most striking of all is the use of a song ('Tell me where is fancy bred') as a hint to Bassanio in his choice of the casket. Mr. Noble points out that the importance of this song has been curiously overlooked, not only by producers ('from whom', he says with justifiable severity, 'bat-blindness is to be expected') but also by commentators. He attributes the failure not to want of intelligence, but 'rather to the contempt with which it has been traditional to treat the songs, and accordingly when a song, as here, is the keystone to the development, it has passed by unnoticed'.

Readers who think the word 'contempt' is too strong should read the late Christopher Wilson's *Shakespeare and Music*. Of the many curiosities described by Wilson the prize should surely go to Sir Henry Bishop's operatic version of the *Comedy of Errors*. The title-page must be quoted:

The Overture, songs, two duets, and glees in Shakespeare's *Comedy of Errors*, performed at the Theatre Royal, Covent Garden; the words selected entirely from Shakespeare's Plays, Poems, and Sonnets. The music composed and the whole adapted and compressed from the score for the voice and pianoforte by Sir Henry R. Bishop, composer and Director of the Music to the Theatre Royal, Covent Garden.

The amazing thing about this work is that Bishop set no single line from the *Comedy of Errors*. Instead, he drew the plums from other plays—'Blow, Blow', 'It was a Lover', the 'Willow Song', 'Under the Greenwood Tree', 'Come, live with me', 'Take, O take, those lips away', &c. As Wilson says, Bishop's avoidance of the play with which he was nominally concerned is 'equalled only by the manner in which Purcell did not set a line of Shakespeare in his *Fairy Queen*'.

Another oddity mentioned is the fact that in Ambroise Thomas's *Hamlet* the opera is given a happy ending, the Queen, Laertes, and Polonius all surviving, and Hamlet being crowned King of Denmark. Even 'happier' is the ending sometimes played in this work, one that Sir Alexander Mackenzie told Wilson he had once seen at Paris. In this jolly affair Ophelia marries Hamlet, and the Ghost gives them a 'Bless you, my children', with melodrama-musical accompaniment. 'It is a dull thing', says Wilson, 'to be a simple Anglo-Saxon!'

§

Mr. Noble gives ample evidence concerning the ill-treatment of the plays on the musical side. Thus, in the eighteenth century the songs were rarely heard on the stage. They were regarded as interruptions, or as concessions to low public taste, and were often omitted. The producers of the nineteenth century went the whole hog in the opposite direction, dragging into one play the songs from another, and even interlarding a play with extracts from the poems and sonnets. So little was dramatic fitness considered that Lewis Waller gave to the cultivated and cynical Amiens, in *As You Like It*, the comic and uncouth

Owl Song ('When icicles hang by the wall'), from
Love's Labour's Lost; and Granville Barker, in his
production of *A Midsummer Night's Dream*, inserted
'Roses, their sharp spines being gone' from *The Two
Noble Kinsmen*—a song not only entirely irrelevant,
but not even by Shakespeare. Mr. Noble says:

> Such producers would probably plead in their de-
> fence that they had never been told that the songs had
> any special function to discharge, that they understood
> Shakespeare merely introduced songs to please the
> public taste, and that consequently they saw no harm
> in introducing a song on any occasion which appeared
> to demand some cheerful or romantic effect.

But one would expect actor-managers and producers
to credit Shakespeare with the ability to indulge
'public taste' in such a way that the drama was helped,
not hindered.

In some matters of detail and opinion musicians
may be disposed to part company with Mr. Noble.
They will not, for instance, agree that the attraction
of 'Who is Sylvia' lies 'not in its prettiness but in its
humour'. Mr. Noble makes out a case for regarding
it as a delicate caricature, but musicians will continue
to take it seriously, and reckon it as one of the most
delightful songs ever written.

Occasionally Mr. Noble's use of technical terms is
loose. Thus, in his admirable suggestions as to the
musical requirements of the beginning of Act II of
A Midsummer Night's Dream, he says that:

> If 'Over hill, over dale' is sung, then Puck's greeting
> ought to be in melodious recitative, and the Fairy's aria
> ought, by means of modulations, to be brought back
> again to recitative [at 'Farewell, thou lob of spirits'].

As it is clear that he does not mean modulations in
the accepted musical sense of the term, it seems a pity
to use the word. Moreover, any kind of leading back
to recitative is unnecessary. The song should end, and

the music at once drop into recitative. In the chapter headed 'General View', Mr. Noble says some sensible things on the vexed question of the idiom a modern composer should employ, but he makes one statement that calls for contradiction, viz.:

> Such songs as 'Under the greenwood tree' and 'Come away, come away, Death', necessitate the differentiation of the second stanza from the first; the freest rhythm in the world will not entirely surmount the objection to the melody's being repeated, and, if the melody is continued, modulations [varied harmony] will be required to avoid monotony.

And later, discussing 'Come away, Death', he says that 'modern musical practice would forbid the melody being repeated for the second stanza'. Well, the only answer is to refer Mr. Noble to the best settings of both songs. Take first those of Roger Quilter. In each case he will find the same melody used for both verses, with very slight modifications brought about by the needs of verbal accentuation, and with of course a little development and lengthening out of the final phrase of each by way of *Coda*. The fine 'Come away, Death', of Benjamin Dale uses the same melody for both verses, save for one short phrase in the middle. In Stanford's admirable setting of this song we see a good deal more variation in the second verse, but unity is obtained by the use of the same melodic material for the opening of both verses. The only other settings of the two songs I can lay hand on at the moment are those in the recently published *Six Shakespeare Songs* by Castelnuovo-Tedesco (Chester). These are so unconventional that the fact of the composer using exactly the same melody for both verses of each song is pretty conclusive proof of what 'modern musical practice' is in the matter. The fact is, Mr. Noble forgets that a song-writer is not only setting words to music: he is also dealing with a musical form, and he has to produce a balanced and rounded result. A setting that considered the words only would almost inevitably be scrappy as music; at the best it would be bringing in fresh thematic material at a moment towards the close where the ear demands some sense of finality. No composer worth his salt will be prevented by this restriction from doing his duty by any change of sentiment in a second verse. There are subtle variations in rhythm, in pace, in harmony, and in the laying-out of the accompaniment in regard to sonority and tone-colour—all these resources are at his disposal, and they will produce a far better result than any meticulous setting of the 'point-to-point' order.

§

Mr. Noble has much to say that is interesting and valuable about punctuation, but I am not convinced by his arguments as to the original markings having had any relation to the breath-taking needs of the singer. These are matters for the composer; the punctuation of the text has little significance from a musical point of view. Mr. Noble's analogy from congregational singing is weak. He says:

In cases where the congregational singing is good, the stops with which the hymns are peppered are largely ignored, and pauses are indulged in where no provision has been made by punctuation or in the music.

But the stops with which hymns are peppered are mainly commas, and therefore are not necessarily stopping-places. Semicolons or full stops occurring in the course of a line are usually observed, though less markedly than in reading. The pauses that are made systematically are at the end of a line. They are usually so short that they do not impair the sense of the words; the slight rhythmical disturbance they create is all to the good in avoiding squareness; and they enable the singers to take breath, besides showing the phrase-structure of the tune. Speaking of Cali-

20

ban's 'No more dams I'll make for fish', Mr. Noble says:

If the song is sung in other than a quick monotone [monotoning is not singing], the last two lines necessitate heavier punctuation than is contained in the Folio. Accordingly in our text, two commas have been added in line five and the comma in line six has been changed into a colon.

I confess inability to see how the singer is affected by either of these methods:

> (a) Ban Ban Cacaliban
> Has a new master, get a new man.
> (b) Ban, Ban, Cacaliban
> Has a new master: get a new man.

A composer setting the words to quick music would not forget to give the singer time to breathe. Punctuation is, however, of great importance, and it is a pity composers have either worked from badly punctuated editions, or have disregarded the correct punctuation when it has been available. The most flagrant case is that of the second stanza of 'Orpheus with his lute' At least two recent settings by composers of standing treat 'killing' as an adverb instead of as an adjective, and so make an ungrammatical sentence. I wish Mr. Noble had touched on this point, the more so as his own punctuation is calculated to confirm the error. He gives:

> In sweet music is such art,
> Killing care, and grief of heart,
> Fall asleep, or hearing die.

I suggest the following as being less likely to be misunderstood:

> In sweet music is such art:
> Killing care and grief of heart
> Fall asleep or, hearing, die.

Hardly less important than punctuation is the

arrangement of lines. Mr. Noble points out that the following form of the close of 'Hark, hark, the lark':

> With everything that pretty bin,
> My lady sweet arise,

is due to an 'improvement' of Hanmer's, who was anxious to provide a rhyme for

> And winking Mary-buds begin.

The mistake arose from the splitting up of the lines. The Folio gives them thus:

And winking Mary-buds begin to ope their golden eyes, With everything that pretty is, my lady sweet arise.

In regard to 'Come unto these yellow sands', Mr. Noble says that 'great editorial battles have been waged', and he devotes three very interesting pages to discussing it. I take up one point only. Here is the end of the song as it appears in the 1623 Folio:

Foote it featly heere, and there, and sweete Sprights beare
       the burthen.   Burthen disperfedly.
Harke, harke, bowgh wawgh: the watch-Dogges barke,
       bowgh-wawgh.
Ar. *Hark, hark, I heare, the straine of strutting chanticlere*
       cry cockadidle-dowe.

What about that *Cockadidle-dowe?* Mr. Noble disagrees with the New Cambridge Text's giving it to the burden [chorus]. He says that

The burden would be expected to reproduce the cock-crow as naturally as possible . . . and this might involve the song ending on a discord—a thing absolutely forbidden by all the rules, especially in Shakespeare's day, when they were rather stricter than they are now.

It would not be difficult to prove to Mr. Noble that the rule prohibiting a work's ending on a discord has long since had the stuffing knocked out of it. But that is not the point. I am not a Shakespearian scholar,

but merely an old and assiduous reader of the plays,
so I venture on a solution with diffidence: Is it not
likely that the 'cry cockadiddle-dow' is merely a stage
direction that has somehow been incorporated into
the text? Such confusion was not uncommon, as Mr.
Noble shows elsewhere in his book.

If it be objected that the 'dowe' is a rhyme to
'wawgh', I reply that the rhyming *may* be between
'chanticlere' and 'beare'. 'The burthen' and 'bowgh-
wawgh' then fall into places as two short non-rhyming
lines. Here is a suggested version:

> Foot it featly here and there, and sweet sprites
> bear
>   The burden.   (*Burden dispersedly*)
> Hark, hark! bow-wow; the watchdogs bark,
>   bow-wow.
> (*Ariel*) Hark, hark! I hear the strain of strutting
>   chanticleer.
>   (*Cry Cock-a-doodle-doo.*)

§

I wish Mr. Noble had been able to increase his task
so as to include consideration of the old musical
settings, with music-type examples. The only setting
given is that of Desdemona's 'Willow Song', in an
interesting appendix by Dr. E. H. Fellowes. Mr.
Noble tells us that 'in order to grasp fully the significance of the songs', he himself has set all the songs to
music, and on page 24 he says that his opinion as to
the non-Shakespearian origin of 'Orpheus with his
Lute' and 'Roses their sharp spines being gone' has
been arrived at 'as the result of musical treatment
applied to them by way of test'. Is not this a new and
dubious way of proving the authenticity of a poem?
Mr. Noble should have given us particulars of the
working of such a test.

Mr. Noble rightly falls foul of Arne for his settings
of both 'When daisies pied' and 'Blow, blow, thou

winter wind'. The former is a good example of the way in which some composers have set to work with a complete misconception of the character of the text. 'When daisies pied' is a comic song in two senses: first, in its relation to the text and characters, and second, in its refrain. We may be sure that the Elizabethan actor who sang it made the most of the 'Cuckoo' refrain, and that his hearers roared at it. The song is now regarded as a genuine pastoral, thanks chiefly to Arne. 'How completely he destroyed its comic intent', says Mr. Noble, 'is made evident when it is piped, in a bowdlerized version, by children's choirs at song festivals.'

Very slightly bowdlerized, however—merely 'summer frocks' for 'summer smocks'. I have often wondered if teachers have ever been put in a quandary by some bright youngster's wanting to know why 'cuckoo' should be a 'word of fear, unpleasing to the married ear'. And, in this connexion, I am amazed to note that another decidedly equivocal song, 'What shall he have that kill'd the deer?' has also been set for school use.

As for 'Blow, blow, thou winter wind', the fact of Arne's setting having been for generations the accepted one for stage and general use, is the clearest proof of carelessness in regard to both text and meaning. Arne calmly disregarded the refrain, 'Heigh-ho, sing heigh-ho', and he spoilt the life of the verse by repeating lines—not because they needed repetition, but merely in order to make them fit his conventional metrical scheme. This is how he makes the six short lines pan out for his eleven phrases:

> Blow, blow, thou winter wind,
> Thou art not so unkind
> As man's ingratitude,
> As man's ingratitude;
> Thy tooth is not so keen,
> Because thou art not seen,

24

Thy tooth is not so keen,
Because thou art not seen,
Although thy breath be rude,
Although thy breath be rude,
Although thy breath be rude.

Likewise, Bill, fetch me that spike, fetch me that spike, that spike. And nobody surely will contend that the complacent music contains the least suggestion of the spirit of the text. Most modern settings are better, but all more or less fail through the composers' seizing on the phrase, 'Blow, blow, thou winter wind,' and giving a rumbustious setting of the 'Storm King' type. But the song is not a descriptive scena about the winter wind; it is a bitter reflection on ingratitude. Quilter's appears to be the best English setting, though the refrain is a bit too jolly for the sentiment 'Most friendship is feigning, most loving mere folly'. The only setting that gives us out and out the bitter feeling is that of Castelnuovo-Tedesco alluded to above. It is marked *triste*, and nowhere rises above a *mezzoforte*, and despite its frequent dissonance has a strong Phrygian flavour. The pianoforte part whirls along, mainly in *pp* consecutive fifths, with a desolate cuckoo call coming through occasionally. The whole thing conveys such a sense of cold and solitude that one almost turns up his collar and blows on his fingers. Odd, that it seems to have been left for a young Italian composer to show us that this song is far from being a mere jolly chest-slapping pæan of open-air life!

§

It goes without saying that Feste's nonsense song, 'When that I was and a little tiny boy', has had a bad time with the serious critics. Mr. Noble tells us that the Georgian and Victorian editors would have none of it, and wished to consign it to the footnotes as the gag of some low comedian. It is curious that although people are ready to regard Shakespeare as a dozen

25

kinds of great men rolled into one, yet they rarely give him credit for being also a popular playwright who knew how to cater for his audience. What could be more natural at the end of *Twelfth Night* than to bring in a nonsense song based on a comic ditty of the day? We know that it was so, for we find the Fool in *King Lear* tipping a stave of it (Act III, scene ii). It was probably as well known to the 'gods' as any comic song is to-day. Most likely the audience joined in the chorus. Yet I remember reading somewhere that a German critic has discovered in this song a profound philosophy, and has expounded it at great length, with sub-sections on some of Feste's complexes. And Mr. Noble quotes from one John Weiss, a Bostonian of 1876, who regarded it as a homily:

Feste is left alone upon the stage. Then he sings a song which conveys his feelings of the world's impartiality; all things proceed according to law; nobody is humoured; people must abide the consequences of their actions, 'for the rain, it raineth every day'. A little boy may have his toy, but a man must guard against knavery and thieving . . . it is a very old world and began so long ago that no change in its habits can be looked for.

After which, dear brothers and sisters, Feste can do no less than pull a straight face, throw a cassock over his motley, and proceed to take up a collection.

HUMOUR IN MUSIC

WE hear much about humour in music, but we are apt to forget that, strictly speaking, the amount of really humorous music is so small as to be almost negligible. By really humorous music I mean that which is funny, not merely through its association with an amusing text or situation, but in itself. This is, of course, another form of the programme-music question. Detach even the most vivid programme-music from its title, and it may take on a dozen different meanings with equal success. Dissociate the music of the most successful humorous song from its text, and who will laugh at it? Left to itself, it becomes mere music, often of an uninteresting type. Those who deny the limitations of music in this respect are faced with an awkward fact. The test of verbal wit and humour is its power of causing laughter; yet how often do we find a Humoreske, Burlesca, or Scherzo provoking even so much as a smile? Has anybody ever heard more than a ripple of laughter at an orchestral concert, save when the double-bassoonist has been playing variations on 'Lucy Long'? It is fashionable just now to describe the orchestration of some very spicy modern works as 'witty'. But wit is entirely a verbal quality. A picture may be humorous, because it can show us incident. It cannot be witty, because wit is almost invariably concerned with the discovery of unexpected relations between two dissimilar ideas, and this discovery can be expressed only in words. Take a Max Beerbohm cartoon, for example. The picture itself is merely funny: the finer quality of wit appears only when the few words of text are added. Where pictorial art fails, music can hardly be expected to succeed. An orchestral score can no more be witty than it can be wise.

The only way in which music may approximate
to verbal wit is in some of its uses of enharmonic
change. The taking of a chord in one relation and
leaving it in another is a kind of pun, and therefore
a form of wit. So far as it is a sudden showing of
an unsuspected connexion between two unrelated
keys it has much in common with real wit. Such
enharmonic surprises are not necessarily amusing, of
course. They may be serious or dramatic in effect,
just as a similar surprise in literature may be beautiful
or affecting. At all events, this is the only sense in
which music may be said to be witty, and with the
gradual exhaustion of harmonic resources, and therefore of surprise, this sense will become more and more
restricted.

But if music cannot be humorous or witty, it can
be comic, because comicality is a quality independent
of words or ideas. A grimace, a ludicrous gesture,
a droll, indefinite sound—all these may cause roars
of laughter. Similarly, orchestration may be comic
by means of droll or uncouth effects. We hear a great
deal about the humour in Beethoven's music, but it
is not easy to find examples. High animal spirits are
there in abundance, and high spirits may produce
music vigorous or good-humoured, but not necessarily
amusing. A really comic effect is the famous entry
of the drums in the Scherzo of the ninth Symphony.
That this is so was proved to me one day at Queen's
Hall, when my neighbour laughed at it, and immediately apologized, saying that the drums were the
cause, though he couldn't explain how. He had never
heard the Symphony before, and was relieved and
interested on being told that he had laughed in
the right place. The uncouth gambolling of the
double-basses in the Trio of the Scherzo of No. 5 is
another comic effect that never fails to amuse, though
we have heard it too often and are too well-behaved
to laugh aloud at it. (A far richer joke than Bee-

thoven's, however, was the unconscious one perpetrated by the conductors who used to give the passage
to Dragonetti to play as a solo, in order that it might
be quite clear!) But the best of all the amusing
passages in Beethoven is surely in the Scherzo of the
Pastoral Symphony, where the

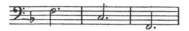

of the second bassoon so funnily hits off the rustic
musician of the type we all know well—the player
who in the difficult passages is busy adjusting his
copy or his glasses, or tuning his instrument, but is
ready to enter with gusto on a bit of tonic and dominant if the pace be not too hot. This seems to me to
be one of the few really humorous passages in pure
music. It is comedy, which is higher than comicality
because it gives us a touch of real life. Even without
the title of the movement to help us, the emphatic
futility of the passage would amuse us almost as
much. And is it too fanciful to suppose that the violas
and 'cellos mock the bassoonist four bars after the
last appearance of the figure quoted above?

The limitations of music are proved by the fact
that composers who wish to be humorous are generally
either (*a*) allusive, (*b*) imitative, or (*c*) bizarre. Allusiveness is not often a satisfactory form of musical
humour. The allusion rarely hits the happy mean
between the obvious and the over-subtle. Here are
a couple of examples. In both 'The Boatswain's Mate'
and 'The Three-cornered Hat' we have

used to represent a knocking at the door. No doubt
this very obvious jest has often been made. Mr.
Glover, for example, is hardly likely to have over-

looked it in compiling his amusing Drury Lane panto-
mime scores, where, indeed, it would be more in keeping than in the two other cases. Moreover, I venture
to suggest that the composer of 'The Three-cornered
Hat' spoils such joke as there is by giving the theme
to a muted trumpet. Introduced as a quotation, and
played exactly as the symphony, it would have been
funnier. The muted trumpet has long since ceased
to amuse us, and its use in this case made the jest
seem laboured. As an example of the over-subtle, take
Stanford's allusion to the 'Die Walküre' fire music in
his song 'Daddy Longlegs'. Now the success of an
allusion of this kind depends upon its immediate
detection by the listeners. Like any other joke, it
fizzles out on being explained. How many of us know
our 'Die Walküre' sufficiently to spot a little quotation
of this kind? But Stanford has scored heavily by his
allusions elsewhere. 'The Critic' fairly bristles with
them. There they are well in the picture, and (with
the exception, perhaps, of the Minuet from 'Ariadne')
are of a type that may be detected by any average
musician who has his ears open.

How often have standard funeral marches been
dragged in with intent to amuse? Parry quotes Chopin's in 'The Pied Piper', and Bridge's part-song 'The
Goslings' has a stave of the Dead March from 'Saul'.
But I fancy that few of us feel quite happy about
humour of this kind. Every audience contains a proportion of people who have recently been bereaved,
and a hundred smiles are dearly bought by the stirring
of one painful memory. The Mendelssohn 'Wedding
March' is much fairer game, and has been made the
most of on many occasions. On the whole, however,
it cannot be said that allusiveness is a particularly
successful form of musical humour.

A much more promising field is that of imitation.
The imitation may be that of sounds ludicrous in
themselves, or it may be a burlesque of serious effects.

An excellent example of the former kind is No. 3 of
Eugène Goossens's 'Kaleidoscope', which gives us a
droll and realistic imitation of a hurdy-gurdy suffering from serious internal trouble. I choose it for
special mention because it is one of the very few pieces
of the kind in which the imitation is so good that the
title is hardly necessary. It has also the power (rare
in pianoforte music) of making most people laugh
aloud. It must be played through at its proper speed
in order to give the joke a chance, but a few bars'
quotation may be of interest:

Here the out-of-tune G's, the way in which the
faulty mechanism insists on striking C♮ as well as B,
and the hiccup of the missing E at the end, are not
merely clever imitations, but capital fun as well.
The burlesquing of serious effects is less easy than
it appears to be. Stanford did some good things in
his 'Ode to Discord', and only failed here and there
because some of the originals were too strident to
be parodied satisfactorily.

§

Berlioz was so much more humorous as a writer than as a musician that we need not be surprised at his failure in attempting to burlesque the oratorio fugue. His 'Amen' chorus in the 'Damnation de Faust' is duller than the thing at which it pokes fun —a fatal ending to what in some hands would have been a good joke. On the other hand, Sullivan's use of conventional recitative formulas is among the funniest things in the Savoy operas. On the whole, instrumental music is most successfully humorous when it aims at creating amusement by *bizarrerie* in scoring or harmony. Such humour is not of the type to set the house in a roar, but it keeps us on tiptoe, and has a good deal of the quality of surprise that belongs to wit. Plenty of examples will occur to the reader, and probably many more are on the way. I doubt if the fashion will be a lasting one, however. It will serve its purpose in lightening our concert programmes, and it will do a good deal in the direction of enlarging technique and means of expression, even though for its own part it has nothing very important to express. The pendulum will soon have swung as far as possible from emotion and will begin its return journey. We shall then find that cacophonous and 'leg-pulling' representations of the woes and amours of puppets, gold-fish, and tin soldiers are evidence, not of musical 'progress' but of spiritual poverty.

The one humorous direction in which music will always be a success is in heightening the effect of an already amusing text or situation. What it can do in the latter respect we have seen in the work of the Russian Ballet. On the whole, however, its greatest scope will always be in connexion with words, because of the facility of performance. A good comic song or vocal quartet can score heavily with the minimum of cost. Why do our best singers so rarely sing anything

amusing? And when they do, why should they choose
(say) a buffo song from Rossini rather than a good
native example, the joke of which is both clear and in
a language we can all understand? Are there no good
British patter songs? Sullivan wrote a few. Perhaps
some day our baritones will forsake the well-worn
Italian examples and show their skill in 'The Sorcerer's
Song', or 'A Nightmare', or 'From Rock to Rock'.
And why do not our choral societies unbend more
frequently? They have no scruples about switching
off from Elizabethan polyphony and making us laugh
with 'What shall we do with a drunken sailor?' or
other droll ditties of a folk-song type. I wish they
would go still farther in this direction and do something to encourage the composers of really good
humorous part-songs. And I am sure that the inclusion of such things in the syllabuses of choral com-
petitions would not only be welcome to the audience
(*and* adjudicators!) but would do the choirs a power
of good. Our singers, whether solo or choral, are not
in need of sobering: some comic relief (with really
good, well-written music) would help them towards
that freedom of style which most of them lack. I remember a choral competition in which the two test
pieces, sung by *eighteen* choirs, were a song about the
loved one being in her grave, and a setting of Henley's
'Invictus', which harped on the words 'My head is
bloody'. No wonder some sorely tried hearers transferred the epithet to the choice of song.

So much modern music is decidedly suggestive of
irony that it is worth while trying to see how this
quality is expressed. Generally speaking, such astrin-
gent tones as those of the oboe, bassoon, cor anglais,
and muted trumpet, with the less expressive register
of the flute, are largely responsible. Such dry and
brittle sounds as that of the xylophone are also helpful. Harmonically, a modal flavour often gives the
right bleak effect. It is odd to find the ecclesiastic and

the satirist joining hands here, but clearly the aloof-
ness of the modes, which makes them ideal for the
impersonal kinds of Church music, fits them also
for use when a composer wishes to get as far off as
possible from emotion. A familiar example is found
in Sullivan's 'Golden Legend', where the sardonic
flavour of the theme usually associated with Mephis-
topheles is partly due to its modal character. The
modern French School will provide many other examples. We find something of the kind even in 'Israel
in Egypt'. When Handel 'conveyed' a canzona of
Kerl's for 'Egypt was glad when they departed', did
he feel at the back of his mind that the wry-mouthed
joy of the spoiled Egyptians was best expressed by a
severe fugue in the Phrygian mode? If not, he builded
better than he knew.

FOUR-HANDED ADVENTURES

NOT long ago appeared a statement to the effect that pianoforte duet playing is gradually dying out. I hope and believe that the writer was mistaken. After all, a pretty safe guide in such matters is the publisher; and when we find (as we do) that duet arrangements of important new orchestral works are put forth almost as soon as the full scores, we may be certain that there must be a market worth considering. On both sides of the Channel there has been during recent years a steady issue of such arrangements, many of them so lengthy and complex that the cost of transcription and publication would be far too heavy an undertaking unless a reasonable sale were assured. This is a good sign, for duet playing is not only one of the jolliest forms of music-making; it is also an invaluable aid to technique and general musical culture.

The pianoforte duet is a comparatively recent thing, for the modest compass of the clavichord and harpsichord gave too little scope for four hands. Burney is generally supposed to have been the first to publish a work in duet form—a set of four Sonatas which appeared in 1777. Grove tells us, however, that E. W. Wolf of Weimar had in 1761 written Sonatas for two performers, which were not published till after his death. It would be interesting to know if they actually appeared before those of Burney; perhaps England was first in the field here, as in some other musical matters. It seems likely, for among the British Museum MSS. (Add. 29996) is a piece by Nicholas Carlton (15—?) called 'A Verse for two to play on one Virginall or Organ', and another 'upon the Sharpe'; and it is now established that the first work for four hands on two instruments was written by Giles Farnaby. After the Burney–Wolf publication the duet seems to have languished, for little was done by any composer of note until Schubert came along with a good stock of works of all shapes and sizes, from full-blown Sonatas to little country dances.

It would be difficult to over-estimate the part played by the duet in spreading a knowledge of fine music. A well-known English composer, lecturing recently on the subject, mentioned that he himself had become a fervent admirer of Brahms after he had got to know the four Symphonies by means of duet arrangements. Similarly, when a very small boy, I got well inside the best Symphonies of Haydn and Mozart by the same means. (Just lately I have been playing those same duets again, and with not less pleasure— rather more.) Incidentally, I recall that my very earliest memories of listening to music in public are of a pianoforte duet, when, scarcely beyond the infant stage, I sat perched on a hard form at some parochial gathering in a small country town while two elderly maiden ladies played the Overture to Boieldieu's 'Caliph of Bagdad'. The pair were a kind of standing dish at such events, and although they no doubt played other duets I can only say that whenever they played to that small boy it was always the 'Caliph'. I recall, too, that they used throughout what Professor Tovey calls 'an elegant hen-like staccato', helped out by constant little sideways darting movements of the head. I remember thinking, as I sat on my hard form, watching rather than listening, that they looked like a couple of elderly hens pecking their way through the music. Peace to them! They gave me my first experience as a listener, and also the only taste of Boieldieu that has ever come my way.

In the title I have called duets 'four-handed adventures', because, in order to get the utmost enjoyment out of the game, one has to use it as a means of exploring all sorts of musical paths that would otherwise remain closed. A couple of kindred spirits,

with fair technique, good reading facility, and plenty
of enthusiasm, can scrape acquaintance with much
of de Falla, Delius, Schmitt, Roussel, Ravel, Casella,
Malipiero, Berners, &c. There is more than a
spice of adventure about the tackling of such music,
though it must be admitted that the thorny progress
is not always well repaid, because so much of the
dissonance that is passable—even effective—on the
orchestra is hideous on the pianoforte. Here again,
however, time is sometimes well and interestingly
spent in experimenting with balance and colour in
order to tone down the worst asperities. And anyway,
one has so few opportunities for hearing most of these
works in the original form, that it is a duty to get at
least a rough working knowledge of them by means of
transcriptions.

§

The technical profit to be obtained from duet playing is so great that it ought to be a regular part of the
young pianist's training. Time-keeping and rhythm
are benefited at once, as in any other form of ensemble
work; ledger lines lose their terrors for the assiduous
duettist, whereas many an experienced soloist is apt
to become a bit speculative when faced with more than
half a dozen. In the matter of resource the hardened
four-hander—that is, the omnivorous devourer of
transcriptions of new music—becomes equipped above
the ordinary. In his adventures he meets with many
a technical hard nut. Does he hold up the march of
events while he tries to crack it? He does not. He
sails along and adapts the passage—a legitimate proceeding, especially in the case of arrangements, for he
is merely substituting a bit of his own transcription for
that of the official transcriber, and it may well be that
there is little loss. There may even be gain. Nevertheless, like most duettists of the ranging, avid sort,
I blush when I think of the shameful dodges to which

I have been reduced at times, especially when playing *secondo*, where of course an unscruplous adapter has plenty of scope. With the left hand kept to its job of carrying on a firm bass, the right can reduce awkward passage-work to its elements, and fill up the gap so that the average hearer is none the wiser. This facility in boiling down and simplifying is well worth cultivating for its own sake. It calls for a ready co-ordination of eye, hand, ear, and brain, and develops a knack of thinking harmonically. But somehow one doesn't want a keen observer looking over one's shoulder at such moments. The resourcefulness is apt to remain unnoticed, whereas the fact that you have dodged a difficulty cries aloud to heaven.

Not everybody wants to keep in touch with the music of to-day and to-morrow; for the unadventurous there are the great things of the past that yield an inexhaustible store of pleasure and profit. Has any musician yet reached a stage when there was nothing left for him in the 'Forty-eight', or the best of the classical chamber music of all periods? Hardly. But we may have few opportunities of hearing them at first hand, and even the wireless and gramophone, boons and blessings though they be, can never (or should never) take the place of performance off our own bat. If there be two of us living in amity under the same roof and unable to deal with the 'Forty-eight' single-handed, there is the duet arrangement made by Dubois—a simple proposition, and one of the best examples of difficult solos becoming easy duets. Less simple, but not forbidding to average players, are the Haydn, Mozart, and earlier Beethoven chamber works; tougher propositions are the later Quartets of Beethoven. (How many pairs of you have managed to 'stick it' right through the 'Grosse Fuge'? Only twice have self and partner reached the bitter end, and we shall never get there again. There are some journeys for which life is not long enough.) The Beethoven

Symphonies seem to make less satisfactory duets than those of Haydn and Mozart. The slender lines of the older men make for clearness, and there is less tonic and dominant brass and drum.

If we are fond of organ music, and get few chances of hearing it (as is the case with thousands of music-lovers who live in centres where there is no good organ or player), we ought not to despise the simple expedient of sharing it with another on the pianoforte. Practically all Bach's organ works can be managed in this way, the *secondo* player delivering the pedal-part in octaves—a humble role, apparently, but in the case of the more difficult and rapid pieces not to be sniffed at. Most of Rheinberger can be played in the same way, and, in fact, all organ music that does not call for the independent use of two or more manuals, or for elaborate registration. (It is worth noting that Rheinberger himself arranged all his Sonatas for pianoforte duet. The only one in this form that I have practical knowledge of is the E minor, which—especially the fine Passacaglia—has given us many an enjoyable twenty minutes.)

§

I have forgotten the name of the old harpsichord virtuoso whose girth increased with his years to such an extent that his youthful feats in the way of crossing hands became more and more irksome, until at last they ceased. A kindred difficulty arises in duet playing when one of the parties . . . However, it is fortunate that Festina happens to be on the willowy side. A duet by an obese couple would be well worth watching, especially in its early stages, when positions have to be adjusted. ('I'm sure you're poaching!' 'Not a bit of it; look! here's middle C. One can't get away from that!' 'Apparently not; I wish you could.' Not a globular duettist among you but has wrangled thus.) Among the minor casualties of life are to be counted those that result from a duet-player not keeping the nail of the little finger of his inner hand cut very close. I have given and taken many a scratch in this way, leading sometimes to effusion of blood, and always to scarification of temper. Reger's arrangements of Bach's Orchestral Suites are the worst things I know in the matter of colliding hands. Nothing if not thorough, Reger seems to have transferred to the keyboard every one of the notes in the score, keeping them all in their original positions. The result is a frequent crossing of the parts, hands getting mixed, notes running into one another, and such fidgety bits as this for the *primo* player's left hand:

where the effect would be better with the quavers omitted.

Reger might well have recast the passage, giving the quaver part to the *secondo* right hand an octave lower, instead of confining that player to the bass in octaves. This is Reger's chief weakness as a duet arranger; he gives the *secondo* pages of octaves, and leaves the *primo* with three (sometimes four) closely-woven parts—an absurdly unfair distribution of the difficulty in quick movements. A typical example of three-part playing, quite difficult at the right speed, is given on p. 41.

The *primo* has to deal with this, while his partner is ambling along with a simple bass in octaves. A lesser man, Ernst Naumann, has done the job better in his version of the 'Brandenburg' Concertos, the *secondo*

40

right hand taking over a good deal of the middle of the texture, leaving the *primo* generally with clear two-part writing. These Concertos are a constant joy to the duettist, especially the lovely first movement of No. 5 in D, and the bustling No. 3.

Too many arrangers of modern orchestral works crowd in overmuch of the instrumental detail, copying rather than transcribing. They forget that musical transcription is to a considerable extent analogous to literary translation. Lots of typical string passages are ineffective, and (in the case of very rapid ones) almost impossible to play when transferred literally to the keyboard. It is a pity that arrangers as a rule show so little courage in adapting such passages. One wonders how many of them have read the article 'Arrangement' in *Grove*, where they may see what Bach, Beethoven, and Mendelssohn have done in the way of modifying string passages when transcribing for the pianoforte.

An excellent move in some recent duet arrangements of orchestral works is the indication of the scoring. This is not only a help in the matter of suggestions for tone, &c., but also an interesting aid to the study of orchestration. For fullness in such indications I know nothing to equal Philip Heseltine's transcriptions of Delius's 'Dance Rhapsody' and 'North Country Sketches'. Everything seems to be shown, and there are also notes giving further information, e. g. 'Strings and W.-W. have the theme in octaves from here to bar 237'; 'Violins (harmonics) sustain two bars', &c. No instrumental detail seems to be too small to be noticed, and the setting-out is clear. Here, for example, is a brief extract from the *primo* of 'Autumn', with a touch of wood-wind on the last quaver of each bar plainly indicated:

For care and skill combined, these transcriptions would be hard to beat, and one readily forgives Mr. Heseltine a few passages where the result seems unnecessarily difficult.

§

The duet *in excelsis* is, of course, the two-pianoforte affair; but that is not for humble folk like you and me. Yet when one thinks of it, there are plenty of us who with great effort (amounting even to overdrafts) have taken to ourselves a grand, when we might have laid out the money to better purpose on a couple of up-rights. They would have taken up rather less space; either of them in an ordinary drawing-room would have sounded as well as a grand; and we should have had at hand the means of making excursions among the Bach Concertos for two claviers, Brahms's own two-pianoforte versions of some of his most important works, as well as practically all the standard concertos, which are to be had with the orchestral part arranged for a second pianoforte. This is the very luxury of duet playing, with the added comfort of being seated in the middle of the keyboard instead of being bounded on one side by middle C. Our diameter ceases to be a nuisance to our partner, and that little finger-nail is no longer a weapon.

Duet-playing on the organ is rare, and for obvious reasons. With all the ample resources at his command in the way of manuals, pedals, and means of duplicating in octaves above and below, one player can do all that is required—even more, sometimes. Moreover, in adjusting oneself to the keyboard, there are the pedals to complicate matters. I once stood by and turned the pages for a couple of players in Merkel's Duet Sonata, and I observed (with pleasure) that there was a good deal of ankle-tapping, and some execution among the corns. With a stoutly shod, clumsy pedallist for partner, organ-duetting may be an ordeal. Are those three Organ Duets by Samuel Wesley still get-at-able? *Grove* mentions them, and also tells us that Julius André wrote twenty-four such pieces, and that one Höpner and the industrious Hesse also tried their hand in this field. But no mention is made of the Merkel Sonata, which is the only organ duet fairly well known to-day. The composer re-arranged it for solo, in which form its native dryness (saved somewhat by the novelty of the duet version) is manifest.

My experiences with long strings of youthful solo pianists at competition festivals makes me suggest that young players should do far more duet playing from the very earliest stages. Apart from the advantages on technical grounds there is the moral effect of team work taking the place of the solo. The duet classes at festivals ought really to be larger than the solo. Audiences are generally much attracted by the sight and sound of a couple of youngsters playing together. Moreover, the musical effect obtainable by two players still in the elementary stage is considerable, whereas singly they make but a poor show. And —a point not to be overlooked—the nervous strain is very slight in a duet, whereas many child soloists clearly suffer tortures.

43

Coming to well-known examples of duets I suppose the Brahms 'Hungarian Dances' are among the most popular. Yet, good as they are, I always feel they would be even better were the *secondo* part lightened somewhat; there are too many of Brahms's thick, low chords. Why do not more players discover Dvořák's 'Slavonic Dances'? I am inclined to put them above the Brahms for all-round brilliance and effectiveness. Again, for twenty pairs of duettists who revel (as they should) in Moszkowski's 'From Foreign Parts', not more than one knows the composer's 'German Rounds', which are among the most delightful of his works. Among recent examples honourable place is taken by the charming little Suite, 'Pages Intimes', of Joseph Jongen, and, in a more brilliant and less subtle way, by the two Suites of York Bowen, especially No. 1, which winds up with one of the jolliest dance movements imaginable. Three outstanding French examples, widely different in scope and style, are the early 'Petite Suite' of Debussy, Roger-Ducasse's very long, difficult and beautiful 'Pastorale', and Charles Kœchlin's 'Quatre Sonatines Françaises'. The modern output, however, is too considerable to permit of anything like a representative list. In the classical field the numerous Schumann pieces are hardly to be beaten: players who know only the 'Oriental Tone-Pictures' should look at Schumann's three other sets, Opp. 85, 109, and 130. I revert to transcriptions from orchestral scores in order to mention John E. West's excellent version of the 'Enigma' variations, and the brilliant transcriptions of Edward German, mostly made by the composer himself.

A recent and welcome innovation is the printing of *primo* and *secondo* parts on the same page. Probably the plan would have been adopted long ago but for the convention that duet music should always be oblong in shape. An upright page lies well within the focus of both players' eyes, and there is the very great convenience of knowing one's partner's whereabouts as well as one's own. In the case of transcriptions of orchestral works, this method of laying-out, plus information as to the scoring, may be of more practical use than a full score. An average musician would be able to study the orchestration, and, if no partner were available, he could take in the music itself, either mentally or by reducing it at sight to a sketch in solo form. Best of all, however, the two-parts-on-one-page form enables you to avoid the delays and irritation brought about by the wretched time-keeping of your partner. Many precious seconds that seem like minutes are spent in counting up bars for a fresh starting-place—'the bar before the *sf* in the third line'; 'But I haven't got a *sf*'; 'Go back six bars before the change of key'; 'I'm in the middle of several bars' rest there.' And so on, with the result that you may be reduced to counting back twenty bars from the end of the page (for it is an almost incredible fact that many duets are published with no sectional letters or figures).

A writer somewhere said the other day that the pianoforte duet is on its last legs, his reason being that such a method of making music is far more interesting to the players than to the hearers. Bless his innocent heart! Doesn't that objection apply to all kinds of music? Apparently he is misled by the rarity of such performances in public. But this is no doubt because there is something a little ridiculous in a pair of players at one keyboard. In a work for two pianofortes one may cut a good—even dashing—figure on the concert platform, but hardly as a duettist. This may be mere fancy on my part. Anyway, I never see two grown-ups engaged in this way without being tickled—and incidentally reminded of the two hen-like little old ladies whom I saw pecking their way through the 'Caliph' Overture. So, although I shall continue my *secondo* activities with vigour, it will always be in private where I can be heard and not seen.

MUSICAL JOURNALISM A CENTURY AGO

MUSICAL journalists too readily and modestly assume that their work has little more than ephemeral interest. Yet one cannot dip into volumes of old musical periodicals without being struck by the large amount of excellent reading they contain. Inevitably this is partly due to the passage of time, which imparts a fortuitous interest to almost anything in the shape of old records. But even when allowance is made for this, there remains a good proportion of capital stuff. It is the custom to belittle the musical writers and critics of the past generation, mainly because some of their verdicts have proved to be hopelessly wide of the mark. When, however, we take up an early volume of, say, the *Musical World*, and read their criticism in bulk, we see that they were more often right than wrong, and are struck by their shrewd and downright judgement, especially in matters concerning performance. On the whole, bearing in mind the fact that their job was almost a new one, they did well. To choose a few of their worst 'howlers', and use them as evidence of the superiority of criticism of to-day, is too easy to be fair. There is plenty of musical journalism written now that is far less able and vital than that of the usually despised Chorley–Davison school.

Musical journals in their early days were little more than pamphlets; the *Musical World* consisted usually of sixteen pages, seven inches by four, and the reading matter in one issue could be got into about eight pages of the *Musical Times* in its present form. (This applies to the earlier years of the *Musical World*. Its pages were enlarged later.) Its first publisher was Alfred Novello, and the contributors included H. J. Gauntlett, Cipriani Potter, Lowell Mason, Samuel Wesley,

J. Ella, Joseph Warren, and Samuel Webbe. The concert notices and reviews are unsigned.

In turning over a volume of this sort one is struck by the familiar appearance of certain discussions and news items. For example: 'The Harmonious Blacksmith' has long been a much debated subject, and in recent years many paragraphs have been devoted to the exposure of the mythical origin of the title. In the *Musical World* of 20 May 1836, we hail the familiar caption as an old friend, and find the myth being started:

A vast deal has been 'said and sung' respecting the beautiful air generally called 'Handel's Harmonious Blacksmith', which is frequently played at the Antient Concerts, as arranged by the late Mr. Greatorex. The indefatigable Mr. Richard Clarke, of the Chapel Royal, St. Paul's, &c., has traced the melody to its right author.

Then follows the time-dishonoured story about blacksmith Powell and his anvil that sounded the notes B and E; and, for the silencing of all doubters, the paragraph ends:

Mr. Clarke has the identical anvil and hammer in his possession, the latter having the letter 'P' rudely indented on the head.

Here is proof enough, surely.

How hardly such fables die! In 1927—ninety years after Mr. Clarke had 'traced the melody to its right author'—there appeared in a daily paper a letter signed J. N. Maskelyne, jun., saying:

Your article on 'Handel and the Blacksmith' interested me because my grandfather, the late J. N. Maskelyne, bought some fifteen years ago an anvil which, he was told, at one time belonged to Powell, the Edgware blacksmith mentioned by your contributor. He discovered that, if struck in the correct manner, the anvil gave out clearly the notes of the familiar theme in Handel's composition.

47

'If struck in the correct manner . . .'—a more than usually potent 'if'!

The newspapers recently (1926) reported a case of a man who was able to sing two notes simultaneously, and, in fact, to deliver himself of a tune together with a simple counter-theme. He was not the first on record, however, for the *Musical World* of 1 April 1836, has this:

A DOUBLE VOICE.—There was a gentleman living some years ago, at Bristol, of the name of Stock (we believe), who could sing in two parts at once; moreover, he could ascend the scale with one tone, while he descended with the other. He sang 'Sigh no more, ladies', in two distinct parts; but not the words, of course; the tones resembled those of an oboe and a bassoon, the former produced by the voice (*falsetto*) and the other from the lips.

Yet another hardy perennial: Devices for turning music pages are constantly being invented, but (so far as I know) they are only moderately successful. Inventors were busy with such things in 1836. The very next paragraph to that concerning the double-voiced Mr. Stock reads:

NEW MUSIC-STAND.—In our last number we mentioned that a pianoforte maker at Utrecht had invented a stand to turn over the leaves of a music-book. A correspondent informs us that he saw a most ingenious contrivance about twelve months ago, constructed by a gentleman connected with the General Post Office, of a great mechanical turn, which was admirably calculated for the same purpose.

And a hundred years hence, if pianofortes still exist for ordinary playing purposes, there will still be folk 'of a great mechanical turn' trying to solve this problem.

The period was not without its prototype of our 'international celebrity' touring party. In number after number we are able to follow the fortunes from town to town of a concert party of four—Thalberg;

Mori, the violinist; Fanny Woodham, a soprano; and John Parry, junior, a bass-baritone. And like some 'star' pianists of to-day, Thalberg carted round a special instrument, though whether its maker's name was displayed in foot-long letters is not stated:

The grand pianoforte on which Thalberg played had, we understand, accompanied the party through a tour to the north of England of about 750 miles, to prevent the possibility of his being obliged to perform on an inferior instrument.

In spite of the meagre travelling facilities the four managed to cover a lot of ground. Thus, in one month they gave twenty-nine concerts in twenty-seven towns in the North and Midlands, ranging from Cambridge to Newcastle—an itinerary which could hardly be beaten even now.

It would be easy to multiply examples of this similarity of matter between the musical journals of a century ago and those of to-day. Here is a final one. Unauthorized 'programmes' constantly appear to-day. In the *Musical World* for 3 June 1836 is a first-rate absurdity concerning Handel's Fugue in F sharp minor. It is ascribed to Momigny, 'a celebrated French writer who imagines music to be a language, and that nothing was ever written without having some little romance or descriptive scene attached to it'. One would have thought that the Fugues of Handel were as free from programmatic bases as music could be. Bearing in mind, however, the worst modern examples of pictorial annotation, we are not surprised to find Momigny attaching the following 'little romance' to the F sharp minor Fugue:

A severe father commands his daughter to give up the object on which she has fixed her affections. She, unable to banish from her heart its best beloved, mournfully pleads, 'Ah! dearest father, let me beg your indulgence.' To this the inflexible father replies, 'I will be obeyed'; and while he thus declares his determination, the poor girl appeals to her mother, 'Intercede for me, dear mother.' The progression in the bass admirably describes the growing anger of the father. [What a familiar ring this has!] At this point the different parts become so lively and complicated that the father, mother, and daughter catch only here and there a broken sentence.

And so on, with a wealth of detail that must be omitted on the score of space. To make a long and harrowing story short: papa becomes increasingly unpleasant, while, in canon, 'mother and daughter lament their inability to soften' him. But even a worm will turn, and the daughter at last becomes 'vehement', and 'is even bold enough to mingle with the protestations of her love the bitterest reproaches against her father's cruelty'. What are things coming to?

Father is staggered:

Astonished beyond measure at such audacity, he is fixed in silent wonder. This is signified by the pedal point in the bass.

And the last word, as usual, is with the women:

The affectionate mother now endeavours to lead back her daughter to the duty and respect she owes her father—

who, however, remains silently impaled on his pedal point.

This is pretty nearly what we may suppose Handel felt in composing this Fugue.

Let us be thankful that this 'celebrated French writer' apparently had no opportunity of telling us what we may suppose Bach felt when writing the 'Forty-eight'.

§

Here is an emphatic protest against the inclusion of operatic arias in a Philharmonic concert—a protest which might have been made in connexion with most

50

orchestral programmes until a few years ago, when
economic considerations practically ruled out vocal
soloists from such concerts. (The items concerned
were operatic arias by Bellini, Mercadante, and Rossini, sung by Italians from the King's Theatre, at
which a season of opera was in progress):

The vocal music was of that class which ought not
to be permitted at such concerts as the Philharmonic.
And the audience expressed this feeling by some very
unequivocal marks of disapprobation. It is true that
these Italians know nothing beyond the airs belonging
to those characters in which they have been performing
in the various towns on the Continent; and that it
would be useless urging them to attempt any compositions of a higher character. They cannot do them;
and whenever they make the attempt, an exposure of
their ignorance and inefficiency is the almost infallible
result. . . . The directors compromise the interests of
the Society as often as they engage such people. There
were better native singers in the room, who could have
sung as well all that the Italians know, and ten times
more sterling music than they probably ever will know.
Several persons seated near to us were so irritated at
the vocal selection, as well as at Madame Coleoni's
singing (which was frightful, attributable to her recent
indisposition), that there was an evident inclination to
make a public appeal to the director of the evening.

Would a Philharmonic audience to-day receive
operatic arias (even if the singing were 'frightful')
with 'very unequivocal marks of disapprobation'? I
doubt it.

The reaction against 'The Messiah' as a stock
festival work is sometimes assumed to be a modern
development. Yet it is at least nearly a century old.
Thus, in a report of the Birmingham Festival of 1837,
the account of the concert at which that work was
performed opened thus:

In spite of the assertion that this perfect specimen
of oratorio writing is 'put up only to please a few old

E 2

women', it never is put up but that young and old throng to hear it. The 'old women' were particularly rife on the present occasion, for not only was every seat (8,000) occupied, but 700 tickets were subsequently sold for standing places. People have a trick of running after that which they like, and know to be good. . . . *Esto perpetua* of 'The Messiah', we say—*erit perpetua*, we believe.

Arising out of this same Birmingham Festival was a warm dispute on the question of fees. The *Musical World* published a letter from the chairman of the committee thanking Madame Grisi, one of the soloists, for her donation of £100 towards the General Hospital. On this the editor comments:

This is very well . . . the same compliment, however, ought to be extended to every member of the band, for they, in relinquishing the extra shillings in their terms of engagement, have in the aggregate given a much larger sum; and individually made an immense sacrifice. The chorus singers were horribly screwed down, so much so that many to whom the pittance of remuneration was an object, *walked* to Birmingham, living by the way with corresponding economy.

In the same number was a letter signed 'A Ten-Pounder', asking the Editor to expose 'the unequal manner in which vocal and instrumental performers are paid at provincial Festivals'. He pointed out that Grisi received six hundred guineas for singing at Birmingham; he blamed, not her, but 'those who consented to give her such an enormous sum', and who engaged chorus singers at £6 per head. He had heard also that 'Master Regondi received forty guineas for playing a couple of Fantasias on the concertina and guitar' [at a Birmingham Festival!].

Far be it from him to detract from the merit of Master Regondi; but he protested against that 'talented youth' receiving for a half-hour's engagement four times as much as the orchestral players were paid for the whole of the week's performances, morning and evening, *plus* twelve hours' rehearsal; and he remained, dear Sir, on behalf of his 'brother ill-paiders, A Ten-Pounder'.

His spirited letter brought forth one in the following number from 'Your's obliged, A Six-Pounder', one of the hapless choralists who had been obliged to foot it to and from the Festival, otherwise he would have lost on the engagement:

How the sisterhood of the profession, who are not gifted with legs strong enough to step from here [place not stated] to Birmingham, contrived, heaven only knows. But doubtless by the next Festival, when the railroad will be completed, we shall be reminded of the comparatively cheap travelling, and treated with a corresponding reduction in the terms.

He goes on to speak of the committee's gratuity to Mendelssohn for his new Pianoforte Concerto, and says that it might have spent some money on

. . . saving old men from the alternative of catching rheumatisms upon night coaches, and others from that of sleeping night after night upon the road, sick and feverish with fatigue—or of returning to London *minus* by their engagement.

During the performance of 'St. Paul', he relates, a member of the chorus fell in a fit, and was carried out in convulsions; the victim had come that morning from some distant place, the writer forgot where. The letter ends with a neat reference to the hospital (for whose benefit the Festival was held):

There is, I believe, nothing like fatigue for bringing on fits with those who are subject to them (I thank God I am not so), and thus it would seem that, among the benefits conferred by the Festival on the General Hospital, there is a chance of its occasionally supplying it with a few patients.

As an interesting footnote to this may be added the fact that the receipts at this Festival amounted to over £11,300.

§

Mention was made above of a couple of inventions which evidently failed. The *Musical World* gives particulars of other ingenious contrivances that seem to have come to nothing. What happened to the Glycibarisono, invented by Cotterini of Milan? It was a wind-instrument of the bassoon type, 'and its tones are said to bear a close resemblance to those of the human voice'.

And what of the Æolian violin? This—an invention of Isonard, of Paris—was a violin played by a pair of bellows:

> The performer holds the instrument after the manner of a violoncello; his feet work the bellows (like a knife-grinder) and his right hand directs the stream of air to the string requiring it.

The palm must go, however, to M. Mareppe's 'Automaton Violinist', which seems to have been a real musical Robot. It was exhibited at the Royal Conservatoire of Paris, and is thus described by M. Bruyère:

> On entering the saloon I saw a well-dressed, handsome figure of a man, apparently between forty and fifty, standing with a violin in his hand, as if contemplating a piece of music which lay on a desk before him. . . . I had but little time for observation before the orchestra was filled by musicians, and on the leader taking his seat, the figure instantly raised itself erect, bowed with much elegance two or three times, and then turning to the leader, nodded as if to say he was ready, and placed his violin to his shoulder. At the given signal he raised his bow, and applying it to the instrument, produced, *à la* Paganini, one of the most thrilling and extraordinary flourishes I ever heard . . . with a degree of rapidity and clearness perfectly astonishing.

There followed a kind of Concerto 'in which the automaton occasionally joined in beautiful style'. He

—or, rather, 'it'—then played a Fantasia, including an *Allegro molto* on the fourth string, *solus*. The tone was 'expressive beyond conception'. M. Bruyère felt as if lifted from his seat, and burst into tears, 'in which predicament were most persons in the room'. The Robot went on from triumph to triumph, with 'double and single harmonics, arpeggios on the four strings', winding up with a '*prestissimo* movement played in three parts throughout'.

This part of the performance was perfectly magical. I have heard the great Italian, I have heard Ole Bull, I have heard the best of music, but I never heard such sounds as then saluted my ear. It commenced *ppp*, rising by a gradual *crescendo* to a pitch beyond belief; and then gradually died away, leaving the audience absolutely enchanted.

M. Mareppe then described the origin of the automaton, which he had made in emulation of Vaucanson's flute player; and the company (having dried its eyes) was treated to a peep into the interior, 'which was completely filled with small cranks,' as well it might be. M. Mareppe said that the machine was so well under control that he would guarantee it to

. . . perform within a fortnight any piece of music that might be laid before it. . . . But [adds M. Bruyère] the *chef d'œuvre* is the manner in which the figure is made to obey the direction of the conductor, whereby it is endowed with a sort of semi-reason.

Another *chef d'œuvre* was M. Bruyère's failure to see the possibility of the conductor's direction being neatly adapted to the Robot's performance.

§

Let us take a hasty glance at the reviewing department, which, considering the small size of the journal, was given a very creditable amount of space.

We are reminded of the belated knowledge of Bach by a review of a collection of organ works, 'Preludes,

55

Fugues, Toccatas, and Fantasias, never before published in this country, Book 1,' issued by Coventry
& Hollier. It is impossible to identify any of the
movements, as the keys are not mentioned. Which of
the Fantasias is referred to in the following? Probably
the 'great' G minor:

> But of all the movements that of the Fantasia is
> most wonderful in construction. It is an absolute
> anticipation of almost every modern invention in
> harmony. It is as profound as anything that Beethoven
> ever wrote. The admirers of this astonishing man,
> Bach, will readily believe that we do not over-estimate
> this composition when we pronounce it to be a stupen-
> dous work of genius.

The review ends with the following note—a reminder that for a long while Bach's organ music was
rarely heard in this country on the instrument for
which it was composed:

> The work contains a separate part for the double-
> bass or violoncello, arranged for the pedals by a man
> as remarkable in his walk as the author himself—the
> inimitable Dragonetti.

Thus the Bachite could enjoy the organ music in
his home as duet for pianoforte and 'cello (or double-
bass). 'With this combination', says a review of a later
volume of Bach, 'they are glorious chamber music.'

I like the editorial pronouncement which accompanies the review column in the journal's first issue:

> In starting our work we may as well explain the
> object we have in view under the head of musical
> criticism. It is simply this: to notice such composi-
> tions as we conceive exhibit ability in their several
> branches of the science, and to *pass over* those which
> in our opinion are not calculated to advance the cause
> of good music. It is neither our principle nor our
> interest to polish and point a cutting and ill-natured
> sentence. Any flippant dapper can make an impertinent
> speech, and any jackass a brutal one.

The 'ill-natured' was very well avoided ('shirked' is a better word) in the following notice of ' "Signal Fires", a Song written and composed by THE WIFE OF A DISTRESSED CLERGYMAN':

The simple circumstance of the Archbishop's lady (an accomplished theorist) having subscribed for three hundred copies of this song will of itself obviate any critical remarks we might otherwise feel called upon to offer respecting its simple and affecting beauty.

I wind up this dip into the past with a couple of light paragraphs. By the way, it is worth noticing that the *Musical World* was anything but highbrow or solemn. Throughout there is a leaven of waggishness, sometimes of the mild-drawn brew, occasionally broadening somewhat, as in this John-Bullish outburst:

The Sultan Mahomet has commanded the engagement of sixty musicians from Paris, who are to proceed to Constantinople for the purpose of performing at the approaching nuptials of the Sultana. 'Assuredly [says a French paper] the good city of Constantinople will reach the height of our civilization.' Ha! ha! Because sixty Paris fiddlers are going there! If conceit and stink are to form the standard of civility, Paris will long remain paramount.

We all know that the 'happy ending' has been violently applied to certain of Shakespeare's plays for operatic purposes. Bellini's *I Montecchi e Capuleti* ('Romeo and Juliet') is an instance, judging from the naïve announcement quoted in the following:

Bellini's opera *I Montecchi e Capuleti* was lately performed at Bucharest. At the bottom of the *affiche* was the following notice: 'To avoid the lamentable effect at the end of the fourth Act, Romeo and Juliet will not die.'

Finally, here is an amusing addition to homely instruments of the freak kind:

THE CHIN-CHOPPER OUTDONE.—There is a man, we are told, who goes about to public-houses to exhibit his extraordinary performances on the common tobacco-pipe. He puts the bell-part against his teeth, and holds the small end betwixt the finger and thumb of his left hand; then with the fingers of his right hand he produces really two octaves. The tone is diversified by the expansion or closing of the mouth, something similar to the Jew's Harp. The manner in which he plays 'The Downfall of Paris' is, we understand, very extraordinary, particularly the last part of it, which runs up and down the scale in semiquavers.

The method is not too clearly shown in the paragraph, and my attempt at the 'Ride of the Valkyries' has so far resulted in nothing more than despairing sighs, and an involuntary assimilation of a small portion of nicotine and other waste product, all my available pipes being of the highly-seasoned and incinerated kind. My next practice (with a somewhat simpler work) must await the purchase of a new briar.

'HEARING WITH THE EYE'

THE mere reading of music . . . is more than a necessity; it is a keen pleasure, and, for me, a keener pleasure, in nine cases out of ten, than that of concert-going.

Ernest Newman.

It is fortunate for concert-givers that few people have anything like Mr. Newman's skill at hearing music with the eye, and that of those few probably not one prefers it to physical hearing. I say 'not one' advisedly. A few years ago I should have said 'only one', that one being the late Baron Rothschild, who was well known to be an enthusiastic musician who enjoyed the art through the eye alone. A full score, silence, and an arm-chair, and there was concert-room and paradise enow.

Of course, everybody calling himself a musician ought to be more or less independent of the ear. As Schumann said, he ought to be able to hear with the eye. Schumann went on to demand the corresponding gift of seeing with the ear—that is, the visualizing of the printed page as the notes reach the ear. (A fascinating game, this; try your hand at it when next you go to a concert and hear something entirely new.) But I don't think Schumann dreamt of mental hearing as a substitute for physical. He merely regarded it as a test of musicianship, as an aid to the study or memorizing of a work away from the instrument, or as a means of forming a judgement on a new work before writing a review of it. Every musical journalist whose work includes reviewing has to be prepared to express an opinion of new music without actually hearing it, though I dare say most of us conscientiously make use of the pianoforte in all but the simplest of cases. But even the keyboard is of little use in the case of extremely difficult music

59

which cannot fairly be judged unless it is played clearly and up to speed. Casting my mind back to some complex examples that have lately come my way, I find myself raising my eyebrows on reading Mr. Newman's dictum that any man who 'cannot read with perfect understanding the score of any song, any pianoforte piece, any violin piece, any quartet, any madrigal, or part-song, or the vocal score of any opera' is 'a poor musician'. If Mr. Newman had said 'with fair understanding', and had inserted 'average' or 'ordinary' after 'any', I should have agreed with him. As it is, I can only say that if Mr. Newman is correct many musicians usually regarded as first rate are after all merely poor ones.

Mr. Newman is right in his insistence on the importance of music-reading, not only for the student, but also for the average music-lover. But surely he is arguing from a false analogy when he says:

> It is as ridiculous for him [the average music-lover] to be dependent on other people for his music as it would be for him to be dependent upon public readers for his knowledge of poetry or fiction. He would be ashamed of himself if he could not read Swinburne or Hardy for himself: he apparently feels no shame in the illiteracy that renders him unable to read Sibelius or Mahler for himself.

But the poet and novelist wrote to be read, whereas the composer wrote to be performed. The poem and novel are complete when once committed to paper, whereas the music has no real existence until it is expressed in terms of sound. I can imagine no greater blow to the art than a widespread epidemic of Mr. Newman's preference for reading, instead of hearing, nine works out of every ten. Composers of to-day already put a great deal into the score that fails to 'come off' in performance. Heaven knows, they need no encouragement so far as writing for the eye is concerned. If ninety per cent. of modern works were put through the test of performance before being printed, tons of paper and hogsheads of printer's ink would be saved. (A coincidence: breaking off at this point, and taking up a recent issue of the *Musical Courier*, the first thing that meets my eye is a paragraph stating that recently Percy Grainger 'held extensive orchestral and chamber rehearsals of some of the most daring and experimental of his larger compositions in order to test the exact æsthetic results before submitting them to the engravers '.)

I cannot but feel that Mr. Newman is inclined to exaggerate the pleasure of score-reading. To place it anywhere near the pleasure given by a performance is pretty much like regarding the leisurely perusal of a menu as only a little less enjoyable than the meal itself. If it be answered that the pleasure of reading a menu is largely that of anticipation, I suggest a cookery book as being a better analogy. The pages teem with appetizing terms and details, and, food being a subject in which all are (or should be) interested even to the point of enthusiasm, we have no difficulty in mentally savouring the dishes described. But nobody is content with pleasing the mental palate. The better the dish looks on paper the more we want to see it on the table before us. And I believe that musicians generally feel like that about music: the better it looks on the printed page the more we want to hear it—for after all the enjoyment of music is largely a physical affair: no savage breast was ever soothed by score-reading. 'Orpheus *with his lute* [not with his score] . . . everything that *heard him play* . . .' 'Here will we sit', says Lorenzo, 'and let the sounds of music creep in our ears.' Not: 'Here will we sit, and, nine times out of ten, like Mr. Newman, read the score rather than hear it played.'

No; not for me the Barmecide feast of the cookery book and the score. I will read both with pleasure and profit, but never as a substitute for the real thing, even though cook and musician fall short of perfection. The meal ready or orchestra tuned up, I can only say, with moist lips, 'Lead me to it'.

§

I do not write all this on the assumption that it really matters a great deal whether Mr. Newman's eye can or cannot take in all that he says it can, or that it matters what I think about that comprehensive Eye. But it matters a great deal that thousands of Mr. Newman's readers, having read, are likely to run away with the idea that music can be enjoyed fully without performance. Although I am ready to believe that Mr. Newman's skill in score-reading is far above the average, I hold that there are more factors in the score of a modern orchestral work—and even in many pieces of chamber music—than can be grasped by anybody, though here and there an exceptional brain, backed up by practice, may go a very long way. We know that even in a good performance much escapes a keen ear, aided though it be by the eye following the music on paper.

Dr. G. A. Pfister, in a *Musical News* article headed 'Spiritual *v.* Fleshy Ear' (? fleshly; 'fleshy' is too suggestive of a 'thick ear'), is frankly incredulous as to Mr. Newman's eye-hearing, and makes out a good case for his scepticism. He says:

It is quite as easy to read one line of music and realize it in our spiritual ear as to read prose or verse. But we cannot read at the same time twenty-five or more lines of intricate orchestral writing, especially in quick movements, realizing the harmonies and the tone-colour, *at the speed in which the composer desires us to hear and feel it*. It is a physical impossibility; the eye cannot do it.

The most important point in the above is the reference to pace, &c., and I have therefore italicized the sentence. Pace is, in fact, the most vital element.

The painful reader of a score may take in, at a moderate pace, most of the details—even all of them—but as a result of the effort the spirit is pretty sure to elude him. On the other hand, if he goes ahead and gets the general effect, he is bound to miss most of the details.

Dr. Pfister goes on to quote Hans von Bülow on the point (again I italicize a vital sentence):

'If any one pretends that he can realize a score by reading it silently, then he is simply talking nonsense. I personally cannot do it. I must first glance it through (*einer Ueberblick gewinnen*), then read the lines separately, then study the harmonies, and do it over and over until I almost know the score by heart. And then, *when I conduct it, I invariably discover beauties or faults which my spiritual ear had been unable to detect.*' That was said in a lecture to students and conductors. And we felt that the great man was telling the honest truth. Had he boasted that he could get more or as much out of reading than of hearing it with his 'fleshy ear', most of us, in spite of our great admiration and respect for Bülow, would have said (in our mind) 'Swank!'

Here, I think, Dr. Pfister is hasty. I do not accuse even the most aggressive score readers of swanking; I merely suggest that natural pride in a considerable mental feat is apt to blind them to its limitations.

Mention of von Bülow reminds me of an apposite passage in Wagner's Letters.[1] One would expect Wagner to be able to do pretty well all that was possible in the way of hearing with the eye. Yet when von Bülow sent him the scores of some of his new works for criticism Wagner wrote:

Your compositions have kept me very busy and interested. Yet from the beginning of our acquaintanceship I have felt the constraint of knowing that you expect a verdict from me which it is impossible for me

[1] *Letters of Richard Wagner*, tr. Bozman (2 vols. Dent), vol. i, p. 271.

to give. In the first place how am I to get any clear notion of the thing? You know how abominably I play the piano, and that I cannot master anything by that means, unless I can form a clear conception beforehand; what I get from simple reading is not enough (compared with what I expect) to get an idea of a composition. Now you will admit that your style is of a kind which refuses in every respect to be judged without cogent experience of the impression received from an actual performance of the work.

This was written in 1854, when Wagner was forty-one years old, and we may assume that the orchestral score that he could not grasp fully through the eye was a far less tough proposition than many a string quartet or piano piece of to-day.

§

I said above that a poem was complete when committed to paper, but on second thoughts I am not so sure. There is a good deal of poetry that, like music, doesn't fully exist until it is heard. Plenty of passages will occur to you at once—passages which, because of their euphony and rhythm, can make their full effect only when uttered aloud by one alive to their beauty as mere sound. Dr. Pfister, in the article I have already referred to, tells us that Flaubert said that he could not tell whether what he had written was good until he had heard it read aloud.

A layman where the stage is concerned, I give my view with diffidence; but I believe there will be something like the right public for Shakespeare when we can count on all the cast being, first, audible, and second, able to give us the beauty and significance of speech that we used to get from Ellen Terry, Genevieve Ward, Forbes Robertson, and from that best of Shakespearian clowns, the late George Weir.

So far as the scenic presentation of Shakespeare is concerned give me an arm-chair mental performance every time. I can see in my mind's eye, Horatio, a more delightful Forest of Arden, and a bitterer Blasted Heath than all the scene-painters and producers rolled in one can set up. The text is on another footing. We may say of all poetic drama that it *may* be read and it *may* be seen, but in order to be enjoyed fully it *must* be heard. When the B.B.C. began giving Shakespeare, there were those who pooh-poohed the idea. 'How could one enjoy merely hearing a play?' asked the pooh-poohers. The answer is, that all depends, first on the play, and second on the hearing. The text must be either humorous, witty, poetic, or all three. Given first-rate speaking and good transmission, an ordinarily imaginative listener who knows his Shakespeare can easily visualize the scene and action. Even a non-Shakespearian, provided he has a keen sense of the beauty of language, would find the experience enjoyable and satisfying.

The above paragraph is not dragged in. There is a real analogy between this reading and hearing of poetry and the reading and hearing of music.

I am sure that all of us who have read Shakespeare a good deal have had the same experience. We have felt we were getting all there was to be got out of him—until we happened to attend a performance. Then, if the speaking was at all adequate, scores of passages—sometimes mere brief phrases—suddenly caught hold of us in a way they had never done before. I had read *Twelfth Night* for many years before seeing a performance, and I hope I was all the time aware of the poetry of this most poetic of comedies. Yet my first experience of the play, well acted, was a series of thrills, as familiar passage after passage took on fresh life and significance from the actors' voices.

In much the same way a performance (even one far from perfect) of a familiar piece of music will often reveal beauties hitherto unsuspected. Some years ago a number of musicians were asked by a musical journal to give in a few words their outstanding experience of the season just passed. Dr. Ernest Walker wrote that his most vivid recollection was of Casals's playing of the C major scale at the beginning of a Bach Suite. Now Dr. Walker had seen that scale on paper, and had heard it played often enough to feel sure that it held no further secrets for him. Yet along came a player and showed him that there is more in it than can be seen by any eye—even Mr. Newman's. If it be argued that in such cases as these the effect is largely the result of the intrusion of the performer between us and the composer, I can only reply by asking how we are to be sure that he *is* an intruder, and not an interpreter? I once had an experience similar to that of Dr. Walker at the performance of a Mozart String Quartet (I was so very much younger then that I have forgotten which). The slow movement had hitherto been nothing more to me than dozens of similar slow movements of the period. On paper it was merely a simple tune plainly harmonized, yet its performance bowled me over. Now suppose that I had been content to enjoy it in my arm-chair; I could hear the notes mentally, and I knew what sort of noise a good string quartet ought to make. Yet I should have somehow missed the secret of the movement.

The hearing of music is full of these strange little revelations—so much so, that the older one gets the less one feels inclined to dogmatize as to the merits of any work.

§

At first one feels disposed to sympathize with Mr. Newman's view that we ought to be satisfied with nothing less than perfect—let us call them hundred per cent.—performances; and that, as these are rarely forthcoming, we should sit at home and, score in hand, imagine such hundred percenters. But in this world of imperfection and compromise we have to learn to be content with a good deal less than the whole loaf; even a half, we say hopefully, is better than none. In the matter of musical performances, welcome as the hundred percenter is on the red-letter days when it comes along, we shall be well content if an average of eighty per cent. is served up. And just as easily as Mr. Newman can imagine perfection, so the rest of us can mentally make up the shortcomings of a performer, so long as he is not so bad as to be distracting. We do the same thing constantly in other departments of music. For example, you are not a gramophonist very long before you easily acquire the knack of turning a deaf ear to any surface noise; and a little later you find yourself mentally supplying deficiencies in the clearness of certain instruments.

Mr. Newman followed up the article discussed above with a sequel, in which he toyed with the notion that, as all instruments are imperfect, the time may come when composers will rebel at this or that note, shake, or colour being impossible on certain instruments, and will boldly write music in which limitations of the kind are disregarded. In other words, they will write, not for performance, but for the score reader. But it is one of the commonplaces of musical history that many beautiful effects had their origin in these very limitations. Mr. Newman says:

No longer would he [the composer] have to submit to the clarinet throwing up the sponge when it reaches the lowest note of its compass and handing over the continuation of the theme downwards to the bassoon. No longer would he have to take the theme out of the hands of one instrument at a certain point and give it to another, merely because at that point the first instrument, though it may have the notes, enters with them upon its 'ineffective' pitch.

We should feel disposed to sympathize with composers did we not know that some of the most engaging effects in orchestral music are obtained from this handing over of a theme from one instrument to another. It began by being a drawback, but composers soon saw its potentialities, and have long since changed the liability into an asset. The number of passages in modern scores that annoy us by drawing attention to the limitations of the instruments is negligible beside those in which the sharing of passages between them is a delight to all concerned. Even the 'ineffective pitches' themselves have been used to good effect for special purposes. And what did Beethoven do when faced with the restrictions of the pianoforte keyboard of his day? Occasionally he succumbed to them, but at other times he turned them to such account that to-day, when the increased range enables us to play certain passages as he would undoubtedly have written them had the keyboard allowed, we prefer the effect that resulted from the restricted compass—e. g. the inverted pedal in the D minor Sonata:

We bless the short keyboard that led to such a delightful makeshift as the above; and it would not be difficult to produce similar examples from almost every kind of music. Genius thrives on such limitations, while mediocrity is for ever complaining of its tools. Take your double-basses down six more notes and the charlatan will imagine he shows daring and originality by writing a passage that calls for a seventh. Carry up your pianoforte keyboard another octave, and some insatiable ass will always want another semitone.

68

Any one who suggests, even jocosely, the writing of music for the eye, must not overlook the fact that such music already exists. Sometimes composers have written for both eye and ear—for examples, see some of the naïve devices of the pietistic composers of early days. Bach himself—great child that he was in some ways—did this sort of thing. The chorale preludes contain many instances. Sometimes the effect is almost entirely for the eye, e.g., the scourging theme in the *St. John* Passion doesn't *sound* like a blow; it *looks* like the convolutions of a lash.

Some of the early writers turned out canons that were marvels of ingenuity, but the canonic structure could not be heard; it had to be looked for, literally. No ear can grasp some of their simultaneous uses of augmentation, diminution, inversion, &c. In his *Double Counterpoint and Canon* Prout quotes a Canon 36 in 1, for nine choirs, by Michielli Romano. The eye sees the three dozen parts busily keeping the pot a-boiling, but all that reaches the ear is an interminable chord of G. Similarly, much of Tallis's famous Motet for forty voices is eye-music. There is even a Bach masterpiece that to some extent must be placed in this forbidding class. The *Art of Fugue* contains some music that clearly was never intended to be played. Fugues 12 and 13 are double-barrelled affairs; in each case the second barrel, so to speak, consists of an entire inversion of the first. Bach bracketed the inversions with the originals, so that his feat may be seen at a glance and followed in detail by those interested, but the two forms cannot be played simultaneously. As their relationship is not apparent when they are played separately, they belong to the order of music written for the eye alone. I showed them to an American friend recently. 'Gee!' he said, 'Gee! for the la-a-nd's sake look at that!'—a comment which leaves something to be desired when applied to ordinary music, but which just meets the case here.

Bach wrote this astounding complication to be looked at, and nothing further.

Probably few things in music are more puzzling to the layman than the musician's power of mentally reading and hearing a score, or even a simple pianoforte piece. The best reply to his question as to how it is done is to show him that he is constantly performing a similar feat. There may be such a puzzled layman reading this paragraph. If so, I point out to him that he is able to hear in his mind the pronunciation of every word he is reading. The words are made up of combinations of sounds; even a word of one syllable may contain several distinct sounds—k-i-n-g, for example, contains four—just as a simple chord is compounded of several notes. The musician's ability to look at a piece of new music and hear it mentally is no more miraculous than the ease with which you, Sir (I address the Puzzled Layman), are now able to hear in your mind the sounds of the words you are reading. No more miraculous? On second thoughts, let us say it is no less.

SHORT CUTS AND ROYAL ROADS

Is the young musician having things made too easy?
When you and I were youngsters we took our instruction almost entirely as powder: there was little or no
jam to help it down. To-day the jam is so plentiful
and the dose of powder so tiny and so carefully hidden,
that children swallow it easily and encore it. The
composers, publishers, and teachers who have compounded the deception pat backs, and proceed to
compound some more.

This sort of thing is regarded as a triumph of
educational methods; nevertheless, carried to the
present extremes it is not a triumph but a surrender.

Take the very beginning of things—the learning of
the staff. This not very terrible ordeal is often disguised as various kinds of games, with complicated
and expensive paraphernalia, the worst example being
one in which huge wooden staves and notes were
used, preferably on a lawn. The children built up the
stave and overcame its mysteries by moving notes
about on it. This was an extreme case, but it is worth
mentioning in order to show the lengths to which the
'make it easy' enthusiasts are ready to go.

Yet, after all, is the staff so desperately difficult
a problem for an intelligent youngster who is fond of
music? You and I are average musicians, I hope.
How many of us needed any help beyond a little bit
of diligence and our memory? There were snags, of
course. We began with the spaces, and got on like
a house afire with the treble lot. F-A-C-E—why, it
spells 'face'! Delightful! A-C-E-G was less attractive, but it was not unfriendly, for the letters made
a kind of word that could be pronounced. But with
the lines E-G-B-D-F, G-B-D-F-A our infant intelligence was not met half-way. We had to get our little

71

teeth into the job and memorize them, wondering why the grown-ups who invented music and made so brilliant a start with F-A-C-E did not carry on the good work by thinking of three other nice convenient words.

When you and I overcame this first obstacle we did far more than learn the notes on the lines. We took a good step forward in developing our mind, and an even bigger one in developing our character. Before we were many years older we found life was full of G-B-D-F-A's in school and out of it. Even in the matter of music alone there soon came a day when the elementary stage was left behind, and, both at the keyboard and at the desk, we were up against technical difficulties that could not be overcome without downright hard work. If we overcame them, as most of us may modestly claim to have done, the grit that helped us was the fruit of the tiny seed that began to germinate when we refused to be beaten by G-B-D-F-A. The best and kindest thing we can do for the child is to admit the difficulty of this first step, and encourage him to beat it.

Much of the great mass of music now put forth for teaching purposes is on mistaken lines: it underrates the pupil's intelligence, and too often it is not child-like but merely babyish. If educational composers and writers will cast their minds back to their own childhood they will remember that when they were (say) ten they rather liked being treated as if they were twelve, but they hated anything in the way of games or lessons that seemed to suggest they were still only seven. Now, I think we shall find that any child old enough to read ordinary simple English, and sufficiently musical to learn and sing an average melody of about the degree of difficulty of 'Early one morning' or 'The Blue-bell of Scotland', is well beyond the babyish stage. Yet a glance at some recent collections of songs for children shows that the writers of both words and music seem to be far from clear as to whether they are catering for prattling infants or twelve-year-olds. Too often it consists of a text in the diction of the nursery-rhyme without the delightful inconsequence and associations of those rhymes, set to music quite unsuitable for infants to pick up. Sometimes it is not clear whether the songs are to be sung *to* or *by* children. A case of a bad misfit lies before me in the shape of a collection entitled 'Six Silly Songs for Sensible Children'. The fact of the melodies being set forth in Tonic Sol-fa as well as in Staff Notation shows that the collection is not for infants. But what child old enough to read Tonic Sol-fa wants to sing such words as:

There was a little sparrow who sat upon a cat,
　And pecked all its whiskers away—
Said the pussy to the birdlet, 'You pickey-peckey brat,
　Do you think you're finding needles in the hay?'

And where is the humour, for child or grown-up, of this bar of the introduction?

Again, the cover contains a 'Prelude' explaining the value of various notes. Thus: 'Semibreve. An egg-shaped border with a space inside. We have not asked you to sing any, because they use up such a lot of breath.' Then the 'sensible' child is told that a quaver is 'Son of a crotchet, with tail. (These are often mistaken for tadpoles.)'

The 'Prelude' ends:

All these notes above require rests, just as we do. When the semibreve is resting, he hangs a little black oblong blotch to the fourth line of the stave (or staff) to show that he 's 'out'. The minim uses the same blotch, but in his case it sits on the top of the third line. The crotchet generally uses a pretty curly thing like this ⌡, and when the quaver and semiquaver are resting, they leave their tails behind them on a stick, and pointing to the left. . . . When every one is resting for a whole bar, they borrow the blotch from the semibreve.

Is this an easy way of learning time-values? Regarded as humour, is it likely to appeal to the youngster old enough to be able to read Sol-fa? Will it amuse the parent? I fancy both author and composer are hazy as to whether their knockabout turn is for 'sensible children' or for parents. Such directions as 'With suppressed indignation', 'Inquisitively, but don't overdo it', 'With bravado, but don't let them think you're bluffing', seem to have been written with an eye on the parent. The rhymes are infantile, the music fairly grown-up, and the dedication implies that the singers are of letter-writing age, seeing that they are asked to 'be sure and write to the composers, at the publisher's office, and say how much they like them'—the songs, not the composers, of course. No, this is a bad shot. Sensible children have no use for silly songs. They enjoy nonsense, but nonsense is notoriously difficult to write, and the brand must be far better than this sample.

§

I began to speak of music written for teaching purposes, but these songs caught my eye and made me leave the track. Getting back, I want to put in a word for teaching-pieces of a less 'jammy' character. Do present-day teachers ever make use of Clementi's Sonatinas? I expect not. Yet, at the risk of being greeted with derisive howls, I venture to say that they might do worse. We middle-aged folk were brought

up on that kind of fare. Did we find it as dry as up-
to-date educationists say it is? Speaking for myself, I
can honestly say that I enjoyed the best of the Sonatinas. They gave me in a very easy, sound, and
pleasant form my first lessons in musical construction,
and I am sure I profited more from them than the
average child of to-day does from the overworked
vein of programme music—the stacks of 'Dolly's
Birthday', 'Pussy's Lullaby', 'The Tin Soldier's Tea
Party', and so forth. Moreover, Clementi and his like
wrote music that was the best of technical preparation
for the classics, whereas much of the modern teaching
music is a preparation for no school whatever. The
majority of children are growing up with an impression that any music which has no fanciful title or
programme is dry and exercisey. This means that
when they come to the great things in music, either
as listeners or players, they will have to make a drastic
re-adjustment of their ideas. The 'pieces' that should
have prepared them for their heritage have tended
rather to make them blind to most of its beauty. The
'make it easy' method, with its absence of discipline
and its shirking of mental and moral effort, ends by
making things hard, and the short cut (not for the
first time) proves to be the longest way round.

The truth is there are no short cuts or royal roads
to real musicianship, and the sooner the child has that
hard truth driven into his young skull the better. A
good teacher will get results more quickly than a bad
one because he will see that no time is wasted. Time
saved is time gained, and this is the nearest approach
to a short cut that we need concern ourselves with.

At the risk of being called reactionary and pedantic,
then, both my hands go up against debilitating, make-
it-easy methods of teaching the young. Anything
worth having is worth paying for, in money or in
labour. Make the youngster's tasks enjoyable, by all
means; but at the same time let it be clear that they

75

are tasks. To attain even a good average standard of
achievement in an art is a long business, and young
and old alike must make the best of it. No short cut
can do more than take us round the corner and there
leave us stranded; and even the greatest genius trod
no royal road other than that open to the rest of us—
hard work.

II

But what of the adult who wishes to take up music
from the start? His fingers are stiff, and his mind
unapt to grasp a system of notation full of inconsis-
tencies and complications. I am led to discuss his
hard case because of the recent growth of systems for
the use of musicians in a hurry. Here, for example, is
an advertisement from *The Popular Science Monthly*.
It tells us all about Mr. Wright's 'New Niagara
Method' of learning the pianoforte. The title of the
method is alarmingly strenuous, so I hasten to point
out that it is merely derived from the address of the
inventor—The Niagara School of Music, Niagara
Falls, N.Y. The advertisement opens up a rosy prospect for would-be players who are not would-be
practisers:

No matter how little you know about music—even
though you 'have never touched a piano'—if you can
just remember a tune, you can quickly learn to play by
ear. I have perfected an entirely new and simple
system. It shows you so many little tricks that it just
comes natural to pick out on the piano any piece you
can hum. Beginners, and even those who could not
learn by the old-fashioned method, grasp the Niagara
idea readily, and follow through the entire course of
twenty lessons quickly. Self-instruction—no teacher
required. You learn many new styles of bass, syncopation, blues, fill-ins, breaks, and trick endings. It 's all
so easy—so interesting, that you'll be amazed.

We know all about those new styles of bass. They

occur frequently in dance music, but unfortunately they give one the impression that they are there for the good reason that the perpetrator couldn't manage the old style of bass.

'No need to devote years of study to learn the piano nowadays,' goes on the encouraging Mr. Wright. 'No tiresome scales, no arpeggios to learn, no *do-re-mi*, no difficult lessons or meaningless exercises.' How is it done? Well, there's nothing new under the sun, even at Niagara Falls, N.Y. What is the following recipe but that of the 'vamping tutor' that has long been a familiar object of the sea-shore?

You learn a bass accompaniment that applies to the songs you play. Once learned, you have the secret for all time—your difficulties are over, and YOU BECOME MASTER OF THE PIANO.

—or, rather, a master of the piano so long as the songs you accompany happen to be so obliging as to fit your accompaniment! For Mr. Wright does not want you to be bothered by copies. If you can just remember a tune, he says, you can quickly learn to play 'by ear'. BE POPULAR IN EVERY CROWD, he cries, raising his voice to capitals:

One who can sit down at any time *without notes or music* and reel off the latest jazz and popular song-hits that entertain folks, is always the centre of attraction. . . . Every lesson is so easy, so fascinating, that you just can't keep your hands off the piano.

§

However, we needn't cross the Atlantic for bright ideas in the way of dodging difficulties. I have received particulars also of two home-grown methods.

Here is 'Naunton's National Music System'.

The advertisements of this system hold out promises so lavish that I sent for the preliminary lesson, known as Special No. 1. It consists of a book of music 'that you can play at once. No clefs, sharps, flats, or accidentals. No worry or drudgery whatever.' The music ranges from *Yankee Doodle* to well-known hymn-tunes, 'with brief instructions how to play them in one lesson'. We begin with a picture of the pianoforte keyboard, divided into bass and treble, with 'Lock of Piano' in the centre:

The diagram shows how we divide the piano in the centre, or where the lock is. The top half of the instrument is for the right hand, and the lower half for the left hand, leaving in the centre one white key (known as D in the old style of music).

The division of the keyboard into strictly defined right- and left-hand sections, with poor D left as a sort of No Man's Land, is quaint. I like, too, the idea of the note being 'known as D in the old style of music', a style which, old as it is, is not antiquated, and will be in use when Nauntonism is no more. Next we are shown how to read:

The black lines of our system correspond to the black keys of the piano keyboard, and the white spaces to our music correspond to the white keys. Therefore, in our system, when a note is printed on a line it means that the black key corresponding to that line must be struck. If we print a note between the lines it means the white key corresponding to that white space must be struck.

This is simplicity itself, and if music were never more than an affair of easy tunes of limited range, accompanied by an occasional chord, nothing more would be needed. But even so, the stave used in this system is so extensive as to be bothering to the eye. Twenty lines are used, a widish space in the middle showing the spot occupied by the note known as D in the old system. You take your measurements from him. Here is a facsimile of the opening phrase of one of the pieces:

78

Play slowly. Count 4 seconds or beats in every bar.

	We Count 4	are 1	but lit - tle 2 & 3 4	chil - dren weak, Nor 1 2 3 4

I gather that by the time the pupil has had the fifty lessons that make up the course he will be able to read and play from the ordinary notation as well as from the Nauntonian. As the pupil thus has to master the old system after all, in order to make use of the standard musical publications, it seems to me that he might as well have got on with it at the start.

A synopsis of the fifty lessons appears on the cover of Special No. 1. At the end of the third quarter's lessons appears the following:

At this stage of your progress you will be a most proficient and pleasing player, much in request at all social gatherings for your ability to play at sight pieces, accompaniments, &c., and from memory, being always able to entertain others. There are still greater heights of music however, and lessons 38 to 50 lead you into the highest paths of Musical expression.

After your fourth quarter's lessons:

Your playing is now of the truly brilliant order. You play with the full orchestral effect that you have noted as being a feature of the playing of the finest pianists. Your capacity is such that you can make the Piano as expressive as the voice, portraying the moods of the music, whether fantastic, capricious, defiant, sombre, or sad. You possess the power to sway the emotions of your hearers.

The lists of pieces of music mentioned in the synopsis introduces some composers whose names are new to

79

me. The piece of resistance in the fiftieth lesson, for example, is a *Rhapsodie Originale*, by F. Hurstmonceux. Then there are also works with similarly high-flown titles (*Sonata Appassionata*, *Sonata Romantique*, &c.), by Felix Dubois, Giavoni Carino, José Martinez, Rupert Courtney, Claude Castlereagh, Paul Morowski, Lilian St. Clair, &c.

The last thing I want to do is to poke fun at anybody who brings the joy of music to a host of people who would otherwise be deprived of it. If Mr. Naunton contented himself with claiming to enable hitherto untaught people to give a rough-and-ready performance of simple music, played mainly 'by ear', I should wish him luck. Clearly there is room for something of the sort. But when he claims that his system can make you 'a thorough musician', or that it will enable you to play 'the most difficult of compositions', he is talking nonsense.

§

Let us glance at 'Pianokode', a method that claims to be 'Understood in an hour'. It requires no knowledge of music, and it 'uses no flats, sharps, staves, accidentals, minims, crotchets, quavers, semiquavers, clefs, rests, dotted notes, time- or key-signatures'. It is 'a complete and perfect tutor', and contains seven pieces that 'YOU can play to-day'. I have not space to describe the means by which you are led to achieve those seven pieces at a sitting. I give instead the opening phrase of 'Annie Laurie'. The tune being familiar, you will be able to work out the method on p. 81 for yourself.

It strikes me as being not so very simple. Moreover, there is the fatal defect that the player who relies on it is limited to the necessarily small amount of music that is obtainable in the 'Pianokode'.

As to the time-saving qualities of such systems: it is apparent that everything taught in their first

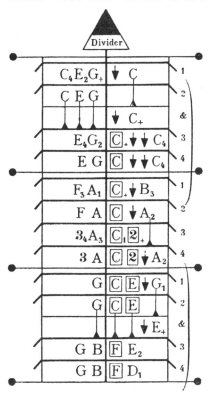

lesson could be acquired easily from the old notation, and almost as quickly—not quite, because the pupil with the old system would be put on to read, whereas Messrs. Wright and Naunton give him nothing but familiar tunes, so that the playing is really 'by ear'. The amazing thing is that thousands of people, young and old, take these courses. A chartered accountant's certificate shows that in a period of three months the number of lessons issued by Mr. Naunton was 50,460! Our chief academies and colleges combined can't show such a roll as that! Nor such an income. Some of the testimonials are ridiculous, but here is one that somehow touches me:

Sixty years of age, and can play 40 pieces correctly

DEAR SIR,—I enclose stamps for that grand piece of music you so kindly sent me, and many thanks for the rest of the music sent to me. I am getting on grand. Sixty years of age, and I can play forty pieces of music perfectly. I remain, A MOST GRATEFUL PUPIL,

Yours truly,

(Signed) Mrs. E. AITKIN HUSSY.

Bless the old lady's heart! I like to think of her playing her forty tunes, and getting on grand. She has the root of the matter in her. I wish she had started on the old lines fifty years ago. If she gets all this pleasure from stumbling through the works of Hurstmonceux and Castlereagh, what would not the great masters have yielded up to her! Of all the testimonializers, she is the only one I can sympathize with. Too many of the others are parents who testify that their children 'play very nicely'. Were these lazy brats mine, they would be smacked into wrestling with G-B-D-F-A, or forbidden the pianoforte. And but for the fact that the adult vampers are beyond the smackable age, I would suggest taking a slipper to them as well—but not to Mrs. Hussy, who is (I hope) still getting on grand, and having a good time with her forty-first piece.

ROBBERY WITH VIOLENCE

ONE cannot attend many pianoforte recitals without feeling that the time is ripe for overhauling our ideas of interpretation, and, above all, of *tempo rubato*, especially so far as it concerns the performance of Chopin. Many eminent recitalists have reached a stage when their studied avoidance of anything like the time and rhythm indicated by composers has become an irritating convention—and one, moreover, that is being copied by the small fry in the domestic circle with disastrous results.

When I saw that a well-known recitalist was to give a Chopin recital at which (it was announced) she would follow the *rubato* rule of keeping the left hand in strict time, while the right fluctuated in pace, I made a point of being present.

The annotated programme led off with this quotation from Henry T. Finck's *Success in Music*:

Rubato means robbed, and it would almost seem as if most of the historians, biographers, and lexicographers, in writing about Chopin's *Tempo rubato*, had been temporarily robbed of their wits. They are impressed, puzzled, paralysed, convinced by the testimony of his pupils that he used to say to them that however much the singing hand might fluctuate in pace, the accompanying hand must play strictly in time.

On reading the quotation, my first impression was that the recitalist wished to show us, on the authority of Mr. Finck, and by her playing, that the dictum ascribed to Chopin was absurd. A ˙note, however, went on to say that she would 'follow the rule in all those pieces which lent themselves to the treatment'.

I have never been convinced that Chopin laid down this rule. Wouldn't it often lead to the harmonic implications of the right hand running counter to

G 2

those expressed by the left? I cannot say that this recital performance shed any light on the question. The player began with the Nocturne in F sharp minor, and delivered the main theme in a distorted rhythmic shape that became more mechanical with each repetition. As nearly as I could note it down, the tune came out like this:

I cannot see that this is an improvement on Chopin's version. In fact, without putting in a plea for rigidly strict time in music of this sort, I believe that an exact performance as Chopin wrote it:

is more expressive and poetic, and even more *free*, than the *rubato* form in Ex. 1.

Again, in Chopin's F minor Fantasia occurs a long-spun melody in quavers, opening thus:

One of the best known of London critics noted down the phrase as delivered by a pianist of high standing. Would Chopin have recognized his soaring melody in the following, with its alternation of stamp and kick:

I have since looked up this matter in an excellent little book by Jean Kleczynski (translated by Alfred Whittingham, and published by William Reeves),

84

How to Play Chopin. The author bases his conclusions partly on information obtained from pupils and friends of Chopin, and we may therefore regard him as an authority. He has a good deal to say about *rubato*. After showing that, so far from being an invention of Chopin's, its origin may be seen in some florid passages of plain-song, he says:

Some of Chopin's pupils have assured me that in the *rubato* the left hand ought to keep perfect time, while the right indulges its fancy; and that in such a case Chopin would say, 'The left hand is the conductor of the orchestra'. Many passages of the Berceuse can be executed in this manner. Paganini also, playing with the orchestra, recommended that the instrumentalists should observe the time, whilst he himself departed from it, and then again returned to it. It is, nevertheless, my belief that this means can be employed only in certain particular cases; and I therefore can only regard it as a *demi-rubato*.

He had previously quoted Liszt's well-known definition of Chopin's *rubato*:

Suppose a tree bent by the wind; between the leaves pass the rays of the sun, a trembling light is the result, and this is the *rubato*.

Somebody else has likened it to the waving branches of a tree, represented by the right hand, the left hand being the stable trunk.

On this Kleczynski says:

There are passages in the works of Chopin, in which not only do the leaves tremble (to continue the comparison of Liszt), but the trunk totters. For instance, the Polonaise in C sharp (Op. 26), third part, measures 9–14; Nocturne in A flat (Op. 32), the middle part. We may quote also the Impromptu in A flat; here everything totters from foundation to summit, and everything is, nevertheless, so beautiful and so clear.

Evidently there is no place in Chopin as a whole for strict time in one hand and free in the other. In fact,

85

the more one goes into the matter, the more certain
it seems that the 'rule' ascribed to Chopin himself is
applicable only in brief sections where the right hand
executes a decorative passage over a left-hand figure;
or in such a piece as the Berceuse, which is an extended example of the same thing, and wherein the
monotonous regularity of the rocking left-hand figure
has significance.

§

Such evidence as is forthcoming seems to show
that Chopin's freedom of *tempo* never degenerated
into the eccentricity of the more enthusiastic ruba-
toists. Moscheles tells us that 'Chopin's manner of
playing *ad libitum*, a phrase which to many signifies
deficiency in time and rhythm, was with him only
a charming originality of execution'.

We see, therefore [adds Kleczynski], that even the
rubato is never a defect in the time; the idea of rhythm,
and consequently *the relative value of the notes*, must
never be lost, apparent changes and momentary incongruities notwithstanding.

I have italicized the words that seem to contain the
whole matter in a nutshell. The trouble with most
of the *ad libitum* playing of to-day is that it destroys
this relative value of the notes, and with it the rhythm.
Kleczynski goes into the question at too great length
for further quotation here. I can only say that he
shows *rubato* to be merely the application of the
ordinary laws of good and sensitive phrasing. It is
not, as many people suppose, something that belongs
almost exclusively to Chopin's works, though naturally there is greater scope for it in his music, with its
highly-organized melodic line, than in (say) polyphonic writing, or in works of a straightforward
rhythmic character. Yet lots of eminent pianists turn
it on indiscriminately. I recently heard, on a player-
piano, performances by a dozen of the most famous

pianists of to-day, and had difficulty in sitting through some Bach and Beethoven pieces in which scarcely a bar was without a hold-up. It was maddening to feel that the culprits were beyond reach of an injunction to 'Get on with it'. By the way, Kleczynski puts forward as an explanation of the non-success of Chopin's E minor Concerto, the view that '*rubato* is applicable only to somewhat short movements; applied to longer compositions it might become monotonous'. Be that as it may, the remark is a useful reminder that excessive freedom can become as uninteresting as too much regularity; moreover, of the two faults, it is the less likely to give us the composer's message, especially in the case of the early classics.

§

After the above was written I was naturally pleased to find my contentions supported by no less an authority than Professor Tobias Matthay in his book, *Musical Interpretation* (Joseph Williams). As he devotes about fifty pages to the subject, with copious music-type illustrations, his discussion of this important element in musical performance is probably the most thorough that has been written. He shows clearly that what often passes for *rubato* is merely eccentric and slovenly *tempo*. I quote one or two sentences from his introductory remarks:

Remember, every time you change the *tempo*, your listener has to start afresh with you, and has to readjust himself to the new *tempo*. This engenders a complete disorganization of the piece if it is a continuous composition; and if this varying of the *tempo* is persisted in, not only does it lead to discomfort, but to positive irritation, although the listener may remain unaware of the actual cause of his troubles.

A simple cure in this case is to make your pupil walk round the room several times, and to insist on his suddenly altering his gait-tempo every few steps.

87

This will make him look and feel such a lunatic, that he will remember the lesson for the rest of his days. . . .

Often enough I hear of teachers who tell their pupils they 'must not play *rubato*'. Such teachers find themselves compelled to take this step, simply because their pupils have not been correctly shown *how* to keep time, nor the real significance of *Rubato*; and because these pupils therefore play absurdly meaningless *ritardos* and *accellerandos*, in place of the required musically helpful and true *Rubatos*.

Again, it seems incredible that any musician in his senses could make the absurd mistake of supposing that *Rubato* implies any *breaking* of time. Yet I know of a number of instances where quite well-known professors deliberately tell their pupils: '*You must not play Chopin in time!*'

Although Professor Matthay was writing with the ordinary teacher and pupil in view, his counsel in this matter is far more needed by many recitalists, the more so as the tyro's interpretative exaggerations are usually copied from what he hears in the concert-room. In his book, *The Borderland of Music and Psychology*, Frank Howes pillories (rightly) the playing of four organists in the matter of *tempo*, giving in notation the actual distortions, registered by some scientific means. But organists are old (almost licensed) offenders in this way, and they have at least some excuse in the unrhythmical nature of their instrument, and perhaps even more in the conditions of much of their work—accompanying a widely dispersed and unconducted crowd, &c. But there is no excuse for pianistic stars, and it is time some powerful critic started a crusade on behalf of sanity and balance. No doubt the unrhythmical and eccentric playing of famous pianists is largely due to their constant repetition of familiar classics. Inevitably they are moved (perhaps unconsciously) to seek for means of imparting freshness and variety to material in which they have lost interest. Apart from this, there is the danger of mannerisms creeping in and becoming established. The remedies are (1) a more varied repertory and (2) drastic criticism in the press. I end by giving two further examples, out of the large number available. In Brahms's G minor Rhapsody a good deal is made of a couple of themes in triplets. Here is the first:

I have heard this played in such a way that only a hearer very familiar with the passage could have identified it. I have attempted to express it in notation, but have been compelled to give it up as a bad job. Is such distortion justifiable? Doesn't it pass beyond elasticity (which we desire) into bad time (which we don't)?

The other example from the same piece is, in some ways, even worse. Brahms carries on this figure:

for long stretches, *mezza-voce*, and its significance in the mood of the piece is familiar to all who know the Rhapsody. Clearly Brahms wants a quiet undulation —a kind of throb, and equality seems an essential. This is what one well-known player usually makes of it:

Here the 'interpretative freedom' has changed the undulation into something nearer a galloping horse. The gallop may be over turf, or with muffled hooves, but a gallop it is, none the less; and away goes the mood of the piece. If Brahms had wanted the rhythm ♪♫, wouldn't he have written it? Had this Rhapsody been for orchestra, or a chamber ensemble, both passages would have been played as written, with no cause for complaint on the score of lack of feeling. The same remark holds good in the other examples I have quoted. Why should not pianists show a similar respect for the clearly-expressed desire of the composer? Can nothing be done to convince them of the difference between free time and bad time? Or must we (like the composers) continue to suffer from distortions cloaking themselves under that blessed word *Rubato*?

KINGS AND QUEENS, ASSORTED

THE time will soon be ripe for a kind of *Almanach de Gotha* of the musical profession, seeing that almost all the available grandiose labels have been appropriated. This particular brand of foolery apparently began with singers of the markedly inferior sex, though it is difficult to say which lady first assumed, or allowed her publicity agent to confer on her, the title of 'Queen of Song'. I have lately amused and depressed myself with making a little collection towards the *Almanach*. 'Britain's Queen of Song' heads the list, of course, but she is now joined by 'Britain's King of 'Cellists', and by Luella Melius, who is billed as 'The New Queen of Song'. But one royalty will soon be of little account: they are now being made by the bunch, one such bunch having recently descended on us from America in 'The Four Harmony Kings'. These Four Kings are alternatively and even more resoundingly known as 'The Monarchs of Syncopation'. The title of Emperor goes begging so far. Perhaps recent happenings are against its adoption, as may also be the case with Czar and Shah. However, there are many other highly picturesque labels used across the Atlantic. Ignaz Friedman has quite a selection, being described as 'the Toreador among Pianists', 'the Colossus of the Keyboard', and 'a GIANT of the Pianistic World'. Curiously, the page that gives the whole set is headed 'This Unassuming Man WORKS WONDERS', though one does not look for unassumingness in Giants, Toreadors, or Colossuses. (No; *not* colossi in this connexion; it is too small a word). However, he is not the only pebble on the beach, for the Chicago *Herald-Examiner* announces that Beryl Rubinstein is 'Giant of Piano'. And so one might go on. Thank heaven that a certain

91

elderly Pole, not without points as a pianist, still prefers to be billed as Mister Paderewski.

The enterprise of the press agent is well backed up by opulence of phrase and flowery diction on the part of some American critics. Thus Vincente Ballester is a 'golden-voiced baritone'; Julia Claussen's voice struck one poet as being 'like soft, warm velvet', while to another it was 'fresh and golden like some great throbbing 'cello'; a third says it 'kept its floaty and fluffy quality throughout', and a fourth tells us that 'at times she subdued her mighty organ to the purling of a brook'. (There is also a reference to her 'handsome appearance' and to the fact that 'the stage was banked with flowers'.) Queena Mario, we learn, 'sings as though she had a thrush in her throat'; a baritone has a voice as 'sure-winged as an eagle's flight'; a conductor is a 'star of the first magnitude . . . 20,000 enthralled as master wields baton . . . this man out of whom flames the power of a Titan', *et cætera*.

The chief point made by one Chicago critic is that 'Rosa Raisa sang one high B flat that alone was worth the price of admission'. It must be remembered, however, that the writer was on the free list and so is hardly a fair judge. We may be sure that if he had paid a couple of dollars, and Raisa had limited her performance to that top B flat, he would have wanted his money back no less than his fellow victims.

Here is another example of absurd exaggeration:

Never has an audience heard notes more crystal clear; never witnessed a more discerning force that gave the interpretation of the Mozart Concerto in A its poetic rendering.

What, never? A critic who remembered that the Concerto has been heard by many hundreds—perhaps thousands—of audiences during the past century and a half, would hesitate before writing such a sweeping absurdity.

One result of the critical style sampled above is

inevitable: superlatives thus lavishly used soon lose
their effect, and what can the critic do then? There
is thus a good deal to be said for the comparative
reserve that prevails on this side of the water. The
press agent of Tito Schipa unwittingly hit on a truth
when to a page of extracts from frenzied critics he
adds:

They Say Such Things As These—And Still There's
A Something in The Magic Voice and Art of SCHIPA
Beyond all Analysis—that Cannot be Described.

Exactly; the dictum applies to all fine performance,
and the weakness of so much present-day critical
writing is that it attempts the impossible and slops
over badly in the effort.

§

Just as I am writing this comes the first of the
seedsmen's catalogues. There are few more delightful
trade publications than these lists, with their vivid
pictures, not only of flowers, but of the hardly less
picturesque beet, broad bean, borecole, and dozens of
other things that make a good kitchen garden an ideal
place for pottering, pipe in mouth. But I mention the
catalogues here because you will find that the seeds-
man has much in common with the more expansive
type of press agent. Ordinary expressions of praise
are not enough, and both alike draw heavily on royal
and other titles. Similarly, just as there is a Colossus
among the pianists, so there is a Majestic among the
potatoes, and the title is hardly more absurd in the
case of the potato than of the pianist—for though a
potato be rich in all the good qualities we demand of
it, it cannot be called majestic. On the other hand,
the naming of a well-known species as 'Great Scot'
was a happy touch; this particular murphy comes
from the right side of the Tweed, and the title suggests
also the delighted exclamation of the beholder on
seeing a potato which the catalogue calls 'very hand-

some, of great repute, round, of somewhat reddish skin, and very prolific'—a description whicn might fit a successful tenor as well as a prize tuber. However, the vegetable over which the seed merchant really lets himself go is the pea. The word 'grand' appears over and over again. Thus, 'a grand old favourite'; 'scores heavily; the flavour is exceptional and is reminiscent of the grand old "Ne Plus Ultra" at its best'. Having given 'grand' a good innings, the catalogue speaks of 'a noble pea', and even more incongruously of 'a magnificent dwarf'. Still, there is some excuse, for with over fifty varieties to praise how can an urgent salesman do other than exhaust superlatives? All the fifty are wonderful, like all the singers and players acclaimed in the American journals. Whence, then, come those flavourless green bullets that afflict the dyspeptic? And those singers that bellow and shriek, and pianists that bang and thump?

'Mother,' said a youngster during a walk round a graveyard reading the tombstone inscriptions, 'where do they bury all the bad people?'

§

However, we must not undervalue the abilities of the brilliant folk whose advertisements are quoted above. Much as some of us may dislike the star system with its barefaced boosting, its limitations on the repertory side, and its frank commercialism, we must not overlook the fact that the real tip-toppers have achieved their position only after very hard work. Nor should we forget that an even greater strain sometimes accompanies the effort to maintain the position so hardly won. Think of the nervous ordeal of almost daily public appearances; of the weary travelling; of a life spent largely in hotels; of the need of being always up to concert pitch whatever one's physical condition; and worst of all, perhaps, the jealousies, squabblings, and petty annoyances, and the difficulty of maintaining a fair and generous attitude towards fellow artists in the same line. There is a world of significance in the anecdote that went the rounds a year or two ago concerning two stars—a pianist and a violinist. I forget their names, so we will call them respectively A and B. They met at a violin recital given by a third star. A packed house was applauding wildly, and the player was excelling himself. 'Phew!' says the violinist to his companion; 'it's getting uncomfortably hot in here!' 'Not for pianists,' replied A. . . .

Let us then give the stars their due, both in admiration and sympathy. At the same time we may venture to suggest to them that less flamboyant methods of publicity would do them no harm financially, and would regain for them much of the respect they have lost among musicians. Do they really imagine that the assumption of such titles as 'Queen of Song', or 'Colossus of the Keyboard', is of any value from the box-office point of view? It is more likely to be a drawback, for there are not a few of us who, resenting the dragging down of the musical profession by such methods of advertising, resolutely stay away from recitals given by self-styled 'Kings' and 'Queens'. No other branch of art is degraded in this way. We do not find Sybil Thorndike announced as 'Britain's Queen of Tragedy', or Seymour Hicks as 'England's Comedy King'. They would gain nothing in appreciation from such announcements, and they would certainly lose a good deal of prestige. There are thousands of musicians no less jealous than painters and actors for the honour of their profession, and the two or three English artists who have allowed their agent to label them in this absurd way will be well advised to stop the practice.[1]

[1] It is fair to add that, by a happy coincidence, the English artist referred to abdicated shortly after the appearance of the above article.

I have already shown that they share such titles with specialists in syncopation, as well as with peas and potatoes. Two further examples should be added. A proportion of costermongers, we know, still celebrate certain high days by bedecking themselves, from peak of cap to the base of bell-bottomed trousers, with buttons. The totals run into thousands, and the hero who can sport the biggest total is known as the PEARLY KING. Last of the list comes the specialist in the more loathsome kinds of bait used in fishing, such as grubs, maggots, and meal-worms (ugh!). One of these merchants used to advertise himself (and perhaps does so still) in fishing journals as 'THE MAGGOT KING'. After which nothing remains but to ring down the curtain with a shudder.

Fig. 1. From the chalk drawing by Kloeber

Fig. 2. From the bust by Schaller

Fig. 3. From the bust by Klein

Fig. 4. From a mask taken in 1812

Fig. 5. From the picture by Mähler

Fig. 6. From the miniature by von Kügelgen

Fig. 7. From the sketch by Lyser

Fig. 8. From the chalk drawing by Letronne

BEETHOVEN: PORTRAITS AND PERVERSIONS

Not long ago these opening words of an article caught my eye: 'On an evening in 1820, a tall, imposing figure might have been seen walking along the chief street in Vienna. . . .' This method of ringing up the curtain took me back to the days when we youngsters read the novels of G. P. R. James, so I went on reading till I found that the 'tall imposing figure' was that of Beethoven—which was quite enough for me: a writer who would say that Beethoven was 'tall' would say anything.

Put this 'tall' legend against the cold fact that Beethoven's height was five feet five inches, and you have in a nutshell the discrepancies between the man and his portraits, both verbal and pictorial.

Beethoven's person and personality alike have been idealized to a degree hard to parallel. Perhaps the most convincing portrait is the chalk drawing by Kloeber (Fig. 1). This shows the composer near his fiftieth year, and somehow gives me an impression of being a good likeness. It doesn't flatter Beethoven with a Jovian front, but there is all the force of character that we know he possessed. I feel I could easily get on terms with this very human person, whereas the Beethoven of the Schaller bust (Fig. 2) makes little appeal. Yet it is a good portrait, if we may believe the testimony of Holz and six other intimates of Beethoven, all of whom signed a declaration to the effect that it was 'a remarkable and speaking likeness'. Probably the substitution of a toga for the familiar coat, neckcloth, and collar, puts us off. Moreover, the disorder of the hair is too carefully ordered.

It is interesting to set against this idealized bust that by Klein (Fig. 3), made in Beethoven's forty-second year. It is free from pseudo-classical trimmings, and has been described as 'the most faithful likeness of its kind'. This is likely, because Klein had the advantage of working from a mask taken in 1812 (Fig. 4).

Beethoven, we know, was no beauty, and any portrait that shows him other than plain—even ugly—must necessarily be false. It doesn't follow of course, that an ugly portrait is right, but the chances are in its favour, so we may believe Klein rather than F. Mähler, whose picture of the composer, aged thirty-eight, is a terrible example of conventional portraiture (Fig. 5). Note the flowing skirt-like garment that tries to hide the disgraceful fact of Beethoven having worn anything so prosaic as trousers—at all events when composing. For that is what Beethoven is doing: Mähler has caught him in the act. The divine afflatus is at work; you see his right hand outstretched with a harking gesture, while his left supports his favourite musical instrument, the *Lyra Spuria*, on which he was wont to try over his symphonies before orchestrating them. By the way, if the composer ever wore linen so spotlessly white as in the picture, it must have been on this occasion only. The temple in the background, and the row of poplars (two) in a neat clearing, add the finishing touches to a picture that ought to be entitled 'Strike the Lyre'—which his name is Mähler. Von Kügelgen's miniature of Beethoven as a handsome youth may also be dismissed as fiction (Fig. 6).

It is pleasant to turn from such artificialities to the well-known sketch by Lyser (Fig. 7). It is usually entitled 'Beethoven in a hurry', but the artist has not contrived to give an impression of haste. The feet look leisurely, and when a man walks quickly, he doesn't as a rule fold his arms behind him. (You *can* walk quickly that way—I've just tried—but it isn't natural.) *Grove* tells us that the composer's friend, von Breuning, testifies to the accuracy of this sketch 'except that the hat should be straight on the head, not all on one side'. It shows Beethoven in amiable mood, and the thick-set, almost squat stature, is in agreement with written descriptions.

An excellent point in the sketch is that, more than any other of the portraits, it gives us an idea of the brilliance of his eyes. Authorities differ as to their colour, describing them variously as black, bluish-grey, and brown; but all alike bear witness to their sparkling vivacity. This feature Beethoven inherited from his grandfather, of whose personal appearance we know little except that he had 'extremely animated eyes', bright and bird-like. Beethoven owed almost all his undoubted personal attractiveness to his eyes and his eager, animated manner when in congenial company. A broad and noble forehead also helped in the conquest of susceptible females—for his life-long friend, Wegeler, tells us that his triumphs exceeded those of many an Adonis. 'What a beautiful brow he has,' said one of his admirers, addressing the company at large. 'Kiss it, then!' said Beethoven, bringing the Brow conveniently forward (an easy matter for a five-foot-fiver), whilst Adonises no doubt fumed in the background.

Yet the women were under no delusion as to his lack of good looks. Thus, Bettina von Arnim:

In person he was small, brown, and full of pock-marks. He is what one terms repulsive, yet he has a divine brow, rounded with such noble harmony that one is tempted to look on it as a magnificent work of art.

And Frau von Bernhard:

He was short and insignificant, with an ugly, red face full of pock-marks. His hair was very dark, it hung tousled about his face. His clothes were very ordinary . . . he spoke in a pronounced dialect, and had a rather common way of expressing himself . . .

no signs of polish . . . unmannerly both in demeanour and behaviour.

He was 'very ugly', said Countess Gallenberg (with whom, as Julia Guicciardi, he had fallen in love); 'ugly and half crazy,' said Magdelene Willmann, the daughter of another of his conquerors; and so on.

Concerning his personal habits, one cannot write fully: even Schindler draws a veil over some unhygienic details. He spat considerably indoors, and did not limit the exercise to his own house. Nor was he exacting in his choice of room in which to expectorate: he was easily pleased, so a drawing-room sufficed. Occasionally, in an absent fit, he would mistake a large mirror for an attractive open space, and . . . However . . .

§

Of the descriptions of Beethoven in company, I quote the little-known one by Sir John Russell, from his book, *A Tour in Germany in 1820–22*:

Beethoven is the most celebrated of the living composers in Vienna, and, in certain departments, the foremost of his day. Though not an old man, he is lost to society in consequence of his extreme deafness. His features are strong and prominent; his eye is full of rude energy; his hair, which neither comb nor scissors seem to have visited for years, overshadows his broad brow in a quantity and confusion to which only the snakes round a Gorgon's head offer a parallel. His general behaviour does not ill-accord with the unpromising exterior. Except when he is among his chosen friends, kindness or affability are not his characteristics. The total loss of hearing has deprived him of all the pleasure which society can give, and perhaps soured his temper. He used to frequent a particular cellar, where he spent the evenings in a corner . . . drinking wine and beer, eating cheese and red herrings, and studying the newspapers. One evening a person took a seat near him whose countenance did not please him. He looked hard at the stranger, and spat on the floor as if he had seen a toad; then glanced at the newspaper, then again at the intruder, and spat again, his hair bristling gradually into more shaggy ferocity, till he closed the alternation of spitting and staring, by fairly exclaiming, 'What a scoundrelly phiz!' and rushing out of the room.

Such traits were glossed over, or entirely ignored, by all biographers before Thayer. When Ries and Schindler projected a joint biography, Ries was in favour of telling the whole truth about Beethoven the man, whereas Schindler stood out for a 'hush-hush' method. As a consequence, they did not collaborate. Yet when Ries later joined Wegeler, he weakened, and became as other hero-worshippers, smoothing over the less-attractive features, and so helping to evolve the fantastic picture of a kind of demi-god that did duty for a portrait till recent times. If a knowledge of the truth hindered our appreciation of the man and his music, something might be said for reticence, on the principle that where ignorance is bliss, &c. But I believe that the more we know of Beethoven's personality, with its mixture of nobility and meanness, the more we sympathize with him, and the greater our understanding and appreciation of his music. A thorough reading of the ruthless Thayer changes one from a doubter into a compassionate enthusiast. The demi-god had left me chilled, even irritated; the intensely human being, with his failings of the miserably petty type, his terrible handicap from childhood, and his afflictions, proved to be one of the most engrossing of character studies. People used to talk about this or that episode in his life as being 'romantic', whereas the real and only romance is in the fact that, despite all his squalid failures and infirmities, he was one of the world's greatest spiritual benefactors. The ninth Symphony and the C sharp minor Quartet gain immeasurably in significance when we realize that they were written by a deaf, diseased, ugly, and uncouth man, and not by the Apollo in Mähler's picture. It could not be otherwise, of course. Mähler's spruce young man would have merely anticipated Mendelssohn, whereas the quality that makes Beethoven's finest music unique is the result of his struggles and falls. Indeed, some of the characteristics that make it so vital to-day are not unconnected with the personal failings concerning which there was for so long a conspiracy of silence. The unrestrained violence that crops up so frequently is merely a musical expression of the fits of rage that led him, for example, to throw a plate of stewed lights ('with plenty of gravy') in a waiter's face, or to behave in the manner described by Sir John Russell. The man and his music have everything to gain from a complete knowledge of his personal character. It is time to shed the false glamour that has so far fogged both—if a glamour may be said to fog. If space permitted, it would be easy to quote passages from Rolland and other writers as misleading verbally as Mähler is pictorially—more so, in fact. Beethoven needs (1) a more frequent performance of certain neglected works; and (2) a resolute avoidance of gush and fiction in favour of a sympathetic study of facts.

Finally, a word on two portraits, one of which was unfortunately never painted. That by Kloeber is my favourite, as I have said. Next to it comes the chalk drawing by Letronne (Fig. 8). One feels that this is a good likeness of the composer before he began to age—which he did very rapidly during the last ten years of his life. It also reminds us that Beethoven in his youth was so swarthy that he was nicknamed 'the Spaniard', 'the Moor', and (by Haydn) 'the Great Mogul'.

The unpainted portrait would have been the most human of all: it would have shown Beethoven smoking. Schindler says that, 'he liked to drink a good glass of beer in the evening, with which he smoked a pipeful of tobacco and read the newspaper'.

Your tobacco-pipe is your true leveller: I have a complete collection of Beethoven portraits, but I would exchange the lot for a simple sketch of the great little man taking his ease at his inn, and blowing a cloud like the rest of us.

BEETHOVEN'S MENTAL POWERS

PERHAPS the anti-Beethoven remarks most frequently heard have to do with his mental equipment. It is commonly said that, apart from his music, he was little better than a fool. The assertion was, of course, a natural result of the exaggerated estimate of his powers as a thinker that held good for a generation after his death. His admirers evidently argued that a composer of profound and lofty music must, *ipso facto*, be a thinker of profound and lofty thoughts. They were encouraged in this belief by the flood of reminiscences and tributes that followed Beethoven's death. He was exalted into a kind of seer; and portrait painters, with both pen and pencil, idealized him into a Titan.

Thayer's biography was a rude shock to the devout. The Titan was discovered to have been on occasion mean, suspicious, and not over-honest. The seer, it was found, had never been able to make up for deficient schooling. His spelling and grammar were erratic; his letters were often barely coherent; his arithmetic had stopped at simple addition. Multiplication was not merely vexation: it was a feat beyond him; all his life he was beaten by any calculation that could not be negotiated by the primitive method of the fingers.

Thayer inevitably caused the pendulum to swing to the opposite extreme, and the present generation has come to regard Beethoven as a kind of inspired idiot—a genius where music was concerned, a mere dolt in every other respect save that of driving a bargain.

But the problem is not nearly so simple as all that. Even a cursory analysis of a big work of Beethoven's shows it to be at least as much a matter of brain as of

heart, as is sufficiently proved by his method of composition. There can be no question as to an extended
work in cyclic form calling for intellectual qualities
of as high an order as those that go to the production
of a fine piece of imaginative literature. Indeed, the
two tasks call for a very similar kind of skill. Like the
novelist, dramatist, and epic poet, the composer of
a long work must achieve a variety that, so far from
disturbing the unity, will actually help it; climaxes
have to be differentiated in size, manner, and matter,
and must be made and unmade in such a way that
every note and every scrap of sound does its bit;
interest has to be not merely retained, but actually
developed up to the close; and the all-round quality
of the work must be so high that, after a few hearings
have destroyed the elements of surprise that captured
us at first, we must be able to go back to it again and
again so long as we care for music at all. Now, the
best of Beethoven's Symphonies and Sonatas, all his
String Quartets (except those of Op. 18), and a good
deal of his other chamber works, fulfil these demands.
Can we question the large share played by intellect
in attaining this result? A purely, or even mainly,
emotional stimulus soon loses its power; it is even
liable to complete failure at any time because it has
to catch us in a favourable mood and in the right
circumstances. The finest music is hard-wearing,
mainly because its composers were hard-working; and
it may be doubted if any composer ever worked so
hard as Beethoven. (As he was the first of the roman-
tics, and did more than any other to enlarge the
emotional possibilities of music, the fact is worth a
moment's thought by young composers in a hurry.)

§

Yet how are we to reconcile the powerful mentality
of Beethoven's best music with his undoubted obtuse-
ness in other matters? The first and most obvious

explanation is to be found in the circumstances of his childhood. His school-days were brief (he was only eleven years old when they ended) and, to make matters worse, he was never able to make the fullest use of his time at school, owing to his father's drastic efforts to turn him into a prodigy.

A boy whose scanty leisure was spent in struggles with the violin and clavier, and who was even liable to be dragged from his bed at midnight by his father and the rascally Pfeiffer (both in their cups) and put through his paces till dawn, was not in a condition to acquire much during school-hours. No wonder his companions found him dull. One of them, Wurzer, who afterwards became an Electoral Councillor, wrote in his reminiscences:

> One of my school-mates was Luis van Beethoven. . . .
> Apparently his mother was dead at the time [she wasn't: she was very busy keeping the wolf from the door], for Luis v. B. was distinguished by uncleanliness, negligence, &c. Not a sign was to be discovered in him of that spark of genius which shone so brilliantly in i i n afterwards. I imagine that he was kept down to his musical studies from an early age by his father.

His association with the von Breunings a little later did much to improve his mind and manners, but the handicap of his first twelve years of wretched home life was too great to be overcome. Only a naturally quick mind could have recovered the lost ground, and Beethoven's was of the slow type, even musically, as is proved by his painful method of composition.

The question naturally arises: If his musical brain was so slow, how came he to be so brilliant in improvisation? All authorities agree as to his sensational success in this branch of art. Those were days when improvising pianists met in not too friendly rivalry: Beethoven played all his opponents off the field. 'He's no man; he's a devil!' exclaimed Gelinek, after Beethoven had met and vanquished him. 'How he

improvises! He'll play all of us to death!' And
Steibelt was so completely floored that he fled from
the room during a hail of notes, and thereafter refused
to be present at musical gatherings unless he were
assured that Beethoven would not be of the company.

But this brilliant improvising is probably less inconsistent with Beethoven's slowness in composition
than it appears to be. All extempore music sounds far
better than it really is, because of the glamour attaching to such displays. Beethoven was a tremendously
forceful player, with an emotional and dynamic range
that took his hearers by storm. It seems to be generally
accepted that the improvisers of that day often took
the precaution of preparing their dashing displays—
a step not unknown in more recent times. (Wasn't
it one of the Wesleys who was discovered 'practising
an extempore fugue'?) In any case, so resourceful a
player as Beethoven must have had at his fingers' ends
a good stock of showy passage-work suitable for all
emergencies. If a reader thinks this suggestion is
unfair, he has only to refer to a couple of Beethoven's
works which are generally believed to have had their
origin as improvisations—the long opening solo of
the Choral Fantasia and the Fantasia in G minor,
Op. 77. Both contain an abundance of pianistic effect,
but their musical value is slight. Even if Beethoven's
improvisations were not all so lacking in originality,
these examples help us to understand how so slow
a composer could be also a brilliant success in extem-
poraneous performances.

No doubt Beethoven's brain was not of the alert
type, and his reported conversation and his incoherent
epistolary style probably make it appear to be slower
than it actually was. The fact is, he was always un-
handy in dealing with words. When he tried to
deliver himself of profound reflections he became
involved and pretentious. His real medium of expression was musical rather than verbal, and his failure

as a song-writer is no doubt partly owing to his lack of feeling for the significance of words. A book, *Beethoven, the Man and the Artist revealed in his own words*,[1] shows this. Judged by these strings of platitudes his intellect would appear to have been a very ordinary one. We have only to compare it with the similar volume dealing with Mozart in order to see a wide difference between the mentality of the two composers. Almost alone in shrewdness is a remark concerning the prospect of an Austrian revolution in 1794:

So long as the Austrian has his beer and sausage he will not revolt.

On the whole it seemed certain that his intelligence was shown in its most favourable light when in company with a congenial friend or two. For example, Friedrich Wieck, in his notes on his first meeting with Beethoven, seems to have found him anything but a dolt. (The interview was, of course, conducted in writing on Wieck's side):

Our conversation turned on musical conditions . . . his own housekeeper, his many lodgings, his promenades, his brother, aristocracy, democracy, revolution, Napoleon . . . the Italian opera . . . my improved method of pianoforte instruction [which was later to produce a Clara Schumann], &c.; all with the most rapid continuous writing on my part (for he asked frequent and hasty questions), and with continual stoppages. For he grasped the whole when I had only completed my answer in part; yet all was done with a certain heartfelt sincerity, even in his utterances of despair, and with a deep inward rolling of his eyes and clutchings at his head and hair. All was rough, at times, perhaps, a little rude, yet noble, elegiac, soulful, well-principled, enthusiastic.

And Sir George Smart, who spent a whole day with him in 1825, found him 'delightfully gay. . . . No one

[1] Compiled and annotated by Friedrich Kerst (Geoffrey Bles).

could be more agreeable than he was—plenty of jokes. He was in the highest of spirits . . . I had a most delightful day.' (Incidentally Smart adds, 'I heard Beethoven say at dinner, "We will see how much the Englishman can drink." *He* had the worst of the trial!')

Rochitz, writing of a meeting that lasted from ten in the morning till six in the evening says:

During the entire visit he was uncommonly gay and at times most amusing, and all that entered his mind had to come out. 'Well, it happens that I am unbuttoned to-day,' he said, and the remark was entirely in order. His talk and his actions all formed a chain of eccentricities, yet they all radiated a truly childlike amiability and carelessness.

Rossini had a short interview with him in 1822. He was depressed by Beethoven's domestic circumstances. ('As I went down the dilapidated stairs I could not repress my tears when thinking of his shabbiness and destitution.') But he gives no sign of being struck by any disparity between the composer and the man as shown by his conversation.

Moreover, although all the evidence agrees as to his eccentricity in conversation, his puns, his rough and at times coarse humour, no contemporary seems to have described him as unintelligent. We have no criticism, for example, on the lines of Johnson's remark that Goldsmith wrote like an angel and talked like poor Poll. Even if such a fault had been found it would after all be no proof of mental inferiority. It is easy to understand that the simple Goldsmith cut a poor conversational figure in the witty circle of a Johnson. Yet the author of *The Citizen of the World*, *The Deserted Village*, *The Vicar of Wakefield*, *She Stoops to Conquer*, and many essays that still make capital reading, was so obviously a wit and poet that the fact of his being, when in company, a fair target for ridicule is not to be regarded as a derogation of his

intellect. The butt proved to be far better furnished
with brains than were some of the wits of his time who
never said (or even did) a foolish thing. The man who
'talked like poor Poll' was a University graduate and
the Admirable Crichton of English literature, so we
must beware of estimating Beethoven's mental equipment by his recorded conversation and letters. Like
Goldsmith, he must be judged by his achievements;
and the brain that could conceive the ninth Symphony
and the String Quartets must have been of uncommon
calibre. In comparison, that of the average successful
business man is a mere bump of astuteness.

§

By far the best of Beethoven's letters, and the most
genuine in effect, are the racy ones, dashed off in haste,
with commas made to do duty for every kind of stop.
There is plenty of good, sound sense and high spirits
in these. You may say the writer was only moderately
literate, but you can hardly call him a fool. But
literacy is a poor test, else a dapper junior clerk would
be judged the mental superior of a thoughtful old
countryman who can do a hundred skilful jobs, yet
can barely sign his name; and who can read both sky
and earth, though apt to stumble over a book.

The more one goes into this question of Beethoven's
mental powers, the more one is convinced that the
tendency is to under-estimate them. That a composer
should be mentally abnormal is not surprising; but
a dull and stupid one is impossible. A creative artist
who is also an all-round cultured man, as handy with
words as with notes (like Berlioz and Schumann), is
an attractive spectacle. But it is easy to conceive of
one in whom the purely musical faculty so far out-
weighs all others as to prevent their development.
Such was clearly the case with Beethoven; and when
we add to this abnormality his limited education, and

the other unhappy circumstances of his youth, we can easily understand his shortcomings in speech and writing. He has been described as a 'magnificent musical instrument and nothing more'. Nothing more! Isn't that sufficient testimony as to his brain-power? If not, heaven send the world a few more such dullards!

BEETHOVEN AS LETTER-WRITER

THE fact of Kalischer's collection of Beethoven letters numbering well over a thousand is often mentioned as proof that the composer was a voluminous correspondent. Perhaps he was, but the Kalischer total is no evidence. (After all, few busy musicians write less than five letters a week, which gives a four-figure total in four years.) Though he seems to have been over-ready to bombard his friends with notes concerning his domestic and other worries, Beethoven held himself to be remiss in regard to correspondence. Thus, replying to a letter from Wegeler, in 1826, he says that 'an answer ought to have been sent with lightning speed'; but, he adds:

I am generally somewhat careless about writing, because I think that the better sort of men know me without this. I often compose the answer in my mind, but when I wish to write it down, I usually throw the pen away, because I cannot write as I feel.

Beethoven's educational short-comings always hindered him from expressing himself on paper. His letters are usually thrown together with little regard to construction; punctuation was casual, a comma being a kind of general-utility sign, doing duty for semicolon and full-stop; handwriting was barely legible; spelling was speculative; and the constant underlining is further evidence of inability to handle words effectively. Add to this that he usually wrote in headlong haste, and it is easy to account for the poor literary quality of his correspondence. Fortunately, the interest and value of letters is almost independent of literary standards; their attraction lies in the extent to which they reveal the character of the writer, and there can be no question as to Beethoven's letters ranking very high in this respect.

In the Preface to his translation of the Kalischer collection, Shedlock says that 'from their general character one is convinced that Beethoven had absolutely no thought of their ever being published'. The best proof of this lies, not in their careless style (as Shedlock seems to suggest), but in the fact that so many of them show Beethoven crooked in his dealings with publishers. Had he thought there was a chance of his letters being hoarded and published, he would hardly have so committed himself. The whole of the correspondence concerning the publication of the Mass in D is a revelation of the curious moral kink in a character that was in many ways so sterling. On this point, by the way, Kalischer is misleading in his annotations. At the foot of one of these shifty letters, he writes:

Simrock, Schlesinger, Probst, Peters, Artaria, and Schott, were all wanting the Mass; the last named acquired it.

They were all 'wanting it' because Beethoven had written to them on the subject, asking them all to keep the matter private, and leading each to suppose that he had received handsome offers from the others, but that the preference would go to the one he happened to be writing to! It is a pity that in the latest edition of the letters [1] Kalischer's notes have not been revised in the light shed by Thayer. Better no notes at all than such examples as that quoted above: it suppresses the truth, and so puts the reader astray. However, let us get away from this side of Beethoven, of which it is easy to make too much.

To the musician, Beethoven's most interesting letters are those in which he discusses proof correc-

[1] Beethoven's Letters, with explanatory notes by Dr. A. C. Kalischer. Translated with Preface by J. S. Shedlock, B.A. Selected and edited by Dr. A. Eaglefield-Hull. (1926. Dent & Sons.) I am obliged to Messrs. Dent for kind permission to quote the extracts in this chapter.

tions of his works. They show that, however much he raged against the task, he spared no pains. He goes the longest way to work, too, and leaves nothing to chance. Where most of us would be content to say 'bars 77–78, tie the bass D', he must needs go thus laboriously round and about:

Between the 77th and 78th bars there must be a tie, which has been left out, namely:

It is here indicated by a *.

This example is from a long letter to Breitkopf and Härtel concerning the 'Cello Sonata, Op. 69. There are about twenty other corrections, all set forth in a similarly laborious fashion.

He was not always lucky in his copyist. Thus, writing to Schott concerning some corrections in the Mass, he speaks of the trouble of going over a score with a copyist 'who scarcely understands what he writes':

I could not find any copyist able even to a moderate degree to understand what he was writing; hence for some of the worst pages I have had new leaves inserted. Frequently the dots are wrongly placed, instead of after a note ⎰·⎱ somewhere else, perhaps ⎰·⎱ Please tell the printer to take care and put all such dots near the note, and in a line with it.

Think of a Beethoven being hampered and hindered by such elementary details! No wonder the sorely tried man fumed. Thus:

The slurs just as they now stand! It is *not* a matter of indifference whether you play

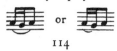

I have spent no less than the whole morning and the whole of yesterday afternoon over the correction of the two pieces, and am quite hoarse with swearing and stamping.

In this same letter (to Holz) he emphasizes the importance of marks of expression, and the difference between the staccato dash and dot:

Now about your copy, my good friend. *Obligatissimo —ma*, the signs p < > &c., are terribly neglected, and often, very often, in the wrong place—no doubt owing to hurry. For heaven's sake please impress on Rampel to write everything as it stands; now only look carefully at what I have corrected, and you will find all that you have to say to him; where · is over the note, there must be no ı also *vice-versa!* ♩ ♩ ♩ and ♩ ♩ ♩ are not the same thing.

There is a lesson for us all in the constant evidence that the tiniest details were 'not a matter of indifference' to Beethoven.

Here is a note bearing on this point. Beethoven is writing to the opera-singer Sebastian Mayer:

Please request Herr v. Seyfried to conduct my opera to-day; I myself want to-day to see and hear it at a distance; by that means, at any rate, my patience will not be so severely tried, as when close by I hear my music murdered. I cannot help thinking it is done purposely. [This was probable, as Beethoven was in a constant state of warfare with the staff at the Opera House.] I say nothing about the wind-instruments, but that all *pp crescendos*, all *decrescendos* and all *fortes ff* were struck out of my opera; no notice is taken of a single one. If that's what I have to hear, there is no inducement to write anything more.

One more reference of this kind: We often speculate as to the standard of performance in Beethoven's day. Apparently there were excellent soloists, vocal and instrumental, but such evidence as is available seems to show that choral singing was backward. In a letter to Breitkopf and Härtel concerning the Mass in C, he says:

In the Sanctus it might be indicated somewhere that at the enharmonic change the flats might be taken away and sharps substituted for them thus:

Sanc-tus, Sanc-tus Domi-nus De-us Sa-ba-oth.

instead of *flats*, the sharps to be kept here

(Nb. ! at B on the same line)

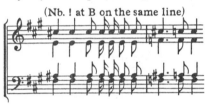

I could never hear this passage sung in tune by our choirs unless the organist quietly gave the chord of the 7th. Perhaps with you they are better—it will at least be well to indicate somewhere that one could take the *sharp* in this passage instead of a *flat*, as here indicated. (Of course it will be added in print as here.)

Probably most singers find Beethoven's simplification, with its ambiguous last bar, more confusing than the original. However, it is now usually printed in accordance with his suggestion.

Beethoven's most famous love-letter is that 'To the Immortal Beloved', concerning whose identity so much has been written—and, indeed, is still being written. Kalischer calls it 'the finest, most wonderful, of all Beethoven's letters, which so often as it is read, touches one to the quick with its glowing words of love and wisdom'. Perhaps most of us will feel that its touching quality lies rather in its blundering incoherence. It was no small emotional crisis that led to such verbal switchbacks as:

Thou sufferest, thou my dearest love. I have just found out that the letters must be posted very early Mondays, Thursdays—the only days when the post goes out from here to K. Thou sufferest—Ah! where I am, art thou also with me; I will arrange for myself and Thee. I will manage so that I can live with Thee; and what a life!!! But as it is!!! without thee.

And again:

However thou lovest me, my love for thee is stronger, but never conceal thy thoughts from me. Good-night. As I am taking the baths I must go to bed. O God— so near, so far!

Yet once more:

Your love makes me at once the happiest and the unhappiest of men—at my age I need a steady, quiet life—can that be under our conditions? My angel, I have just been told that the mail-coach goes every day.

At first the sudden drops from rhapsody into matter-of-fact strike one as bathos; after a bit it is seen that, after all, they are pathetic rather than bathetic. Well might the distraught man say elsewhere in the letter, 'There are moments in which I feel that speech is powerless'. It was so, in the hands of one whose natural medium of expression was music.

The real 'unbuttoned' Beethoven turns up constantly in the Letters, especially in short, hurried notes to Baron Zmeskall, who supplied him with quill pens, and was very much at his service in all kinds of ways. Thus:

Not extraordinary, but very orderly, ordinary quill-cutter, whose virtuosity in this matter has already decreased, these quills need repairing. . . .

Most extraordinary one, we beg for your servant to

find some one to clean out the rooms; as he knows the parish, he can at once fix the price.

But soon—carnival ragamuffin!!!
to Herr von Zmeskall.

The enclosed letter is at least eight days old.

Here is another, dated the same day:

Wonderful, chief soaring man in the world, and that without help of lever!!! We are greatly indebted to you for having bestowed on us a portion of your buoyancy. We desire personally to thank you for it, and therefore invite you to come to-morrow to the Swan Inn.

Damned, dear little ex-music Count, what the devil do you mean—will you come to-day to the Swan? No? Yes.

Puns—mostly bad ones—abound. He cannot mention Traeg without adding that that worthy is slow (*traeg*). Steiner must needs be warned against being 'stony'; and so on.

As specimens of the curt, take the three notes written to Count Lichnowsky, Schuppanzigh, and Schindler, just before the concert at which the ninth Symphony had its first performance. The three long-suffering friends had waited on Beethoven, and had tried to get him to write down definite instructions concerning the event. After their departure, the composer had one of his suspicious fits, and shot after them the following notes:

Count Lichnowsky: I despise falsehoods—visit me no more!

Schuppanzigh: Visit me no more. I give no concert!

Schindler: Do not come to see me again till I send for you. No concert!

It was a good thing for music that these three, like most of Beethoven's friends, consistently refused to be offended by his erratic temper. They simply went ahead with the arrangements, and the concert duly took place.

118

§

Very interesting on the human side are the numerous letters dealing with his domestic worries. Most of these are written to Baron Zmeskall and Frau Nanette Streicher. They give us an intimate picture of the composer's muddled household. Servants come and go in a sort of agitated procession. No wonder, when we read of the composer's violence! Nany was a hussy who seems to have given much trouble: this is what happened to Nany:

The evening before last N[any] began to jeer at me for ringing the bell, after the manner *of all low people*, so she already knew that I had written *to you* [Frau Streicher] about it. Yesterday the infernal tricks recommenced. I made short work of it, and threw at her my heavy chair; after that I was at peace the whole day.

Yet the slut was not unused to being fired at by whatever was handy. About this same time we find Beethoven writing to Frau Streicher:

I have endured much to-day from N., but have thrown half a dozen books at her head as a New Year's gift.

Nany had a lickerish tooth, and was wont to satisfy it by helping herself at odd moments:

As for N.'s *honesty*, I can't say much for it; she likes to pick at dainties, and this may be the cause of it. As soon as the other maid arrives, I will, the first time you pay me a visit, call her in, and *in your presence* express my doubts about the kitchen-book.

The men-servants were no better. Here is Beethoven, in 1817, complaining of one of them:

I hastened back here yesterday morning, but found that my servant was not at home, and that he had even taken with him the key of the rooms. The weather was very cool; coming from town, I had nothing but a thin pair of trousers on, and so I was obliged to wander about, three long hours. This did me harm, and I felt it the whole day.

This year—1817—was a calamitous one in regard to servants:

Again unfortunate with a servant and *probably also robbed* [he writes to Zmeskall]. Already on the 4th I gave him 14 days' notice, but he gets drunk, stays whole nights out of the house, and is so bold and coarse that I would like to send him away still sooner. I should like to pay him the fortnight and let him go his way.

And there follows anxious inquiry as to wage complications: the man's month begins on the first; as notice was given on the fourth, would Beethoven have to pay him for the odd four days if he left (say) on the twelfth?

No doubt this man was the rascal concerned in the mysterious disappearance of a pair of stockings, about which Beethoven writes a confused rigmarole:

I send you the washing, also 11 florins which I still owe your washerwoman. As regards a new servant, I think for the moment, as I have given notice to him, to stick to it. To whomsoever we may ascribe the loss of all the things . . . I hold him rather the thief than any other. I beg you only to say to him that you thought that *a pair of socks had been lost, this is clear from the letter which you wrote to me about it*; he is always telling me that you had found the socks again. The washerwoman received two pairs of stockings, as the *two washing-bills, yours and mine, showed; and this would not be so had she not received them*. So I am convinced that she gave him the two pairs of stockings, as she certainly received them, so that they must have got lost only through him.

What a to-do about a pair of socks, probably darned at that!

As for the thief's successor:

. . . he could enter my service on the first day of next month. . . . If he wants to cook, i.e. for himself, he can use my wood, and as he will still have to go to town two or three times a week, I will give him for that a fitting remuneration, for instance, I will give him what it costs to mend a pair of boots,—

an interesting reminder that in those 'busless and tramless days the cost of shoe leather had to be reckoned with when one lived out of town, as Beethoven did at this time.

Here is another petty thief:

Best Frau von Streicher,

This servant is *scarcely* honest, though I will not *condemn him straight off.* I think, meanwhile, of keeping him still here, with the *housekeeper. What do you think?* It will probably not be easy to find another one at once, and yet I fear the *fellow* might have a *bad influence over an honest person.* I send you here the two keys, so that you can inspect everything. Dusters are wanted—even here, for the devil has already carried off 2 or 3 times my household things.

Other letters show that good cooking was as hard to come by as honesty:

I am still unwell, and there is little comfort in the house; the food yesterday and to-day was really *bad.* This person lacks reflection: more about her when we meet.

Much more, we may be certain.

In fairness to the servants it must be admitted that a new one generally started under the handicap of prejudice. Thus we find Beethoven noting on June 8, 1818, at Müdling, that 'the new housekeeper arrived —troglodyte, inhabitant of hell'!

I said above that domestics came and went in excited procession. That this was no exaggeration is proved by a brief extract from one of Beethoven's note-books:

On April 17 the kitchen maid came.
May 16, gave notice to the kitchen maid.
May 19, the kitchen maid left.

May 30, the woman entered upon her duties.
July 1, the new kitchen maid came.
July 28, the kitchen maid ran away in the evening.
July 30, the woman from Lower Döbling entered
service.
September 9, the girl entered service.
October 22, the girl left.
December 12, the kitchen maid entered service.
December 18, the kitchen maid gave notice.

As Beethoven said in the letter to the 'Immortal
Beloved', 'What a life!'

§

Finally, let us glance at Beethoven *in loco parentis*,
writing to young Carl:

The upper or lower sample for 21 florins seems to
me the best; the landlord can perhaps advise you—
trousers 88—
    4½—
You receive herewith 62 fl., 30 kreutzers, give a correct
account about it. It is earned with great trouble—
however, for the sake of *one* fl. (per ell) it is wiser to
have the best.

For the trousers also the best! However, do not put
on your best clothes when at home. One need not be
fully dressed when anybody calls; so as soon as you
come home, take off your coat and make yourself comfortable in the clothes meant for that purpose.

The wench left yesterday, and has not come back;
the old woman is troubled that she has to go, because
like a wild beast without aim and sense, she cannot
rest. God have pity on me, it has already commenced
with the *cooking* yesterday.

Young Carl was entrusted with all sorts of com-
missions. In a letter dealing with a variety of musical
matters, Beethoven suddenly switches off into kerseymere trousers:

Tell the tailor in the Kärntnerstrasse to fetch the
cloth for a pair of trousers, and to make them long in

the legs, yet without straps, a kerseymere cloth pair of
trousers. The cobbler has his shop in the town, in
the Spiegelgasse, straight before you as you are going
from the Graben. His name is *Magnus Senn*, near the
Town Hall, No. 1090—go to Hönigstein and *be frank*,
so that one may know how the wretch has acted.

There is a touch of reproach in the following. Carl
was evidently spending too much, and Beethoven
recalls his own needy boyhood:

I beg you to bring me some shaving soap, and at
least a couple of razors [Beethoven was writing from
the country to Carl at Vienna], and here are 2 fl. for
the knifegrinder if there is something to pay, if not
for [your] housekeeping; for you always have too much
money—but a Viennese remains a Viennese. I was
glad when I could help my poor parents; what a difference in my behaviour to you, and yours to me—
thoughtless fellow, farewell.

You faithful Father.

Bring anything in the shape of a newspaper with you.

What a picture all these letters give us of a genius
wasting his time, nerves, and energy over a thousand
things that ought never to have concerned him at all!
One cannot but speculate as to the number of masterpieces that the world missed for no better reason than
that Beethoven failed to find a good, sensible, mana-
ging wife. His life would no doubt have been prolonged (and that of his wife as probably shortened)
and a fruitful fourth period would have enriched the
world.

The reader who wishes to get a real view of Beethoven the man should dip into the correspondence.
The style may put him off at first; but in the end he
will not wish a single eccentricity, irrelevance, pun,
or rough jest, pruned away or watered down. It is
doubtful if any letters in existence give a more faithful
self-portrait than these of Beethoven. They leave one
far more in sympathy with the composer than the

highfalutin eulogies that for so long were the fashion. Beethoven biographies, of all shapes and sizes, will no doubt continue to be written, and, for the sake of chronology, they will have a certain value. But all the biographies lumped together can give us no truer picture of the man than he unconsciously gives us himself in his letters and music.

BROWS, HIGH AND LOW

THE question of popular taste never goes long without
an airing, and sooner or later we are told that a big
sale is a proof of merit. This view, put forward by
the purveyors of rubbish, is of course easily knocked
on the head by a glance at almost any one of the
popular successes of the moment. For example, 'Yes,
we have no bananas' had a staggering sale and made
the fortunes of the little group of men who inflicted
it on us. Yet nobody has been known to defend—
much less praise—either words or music. Why then
did we succumb to it? The answer is important,
because it explains the vogue of nine-tenths of the
'best-sellers', and shows that the question of quality
scarcely enters into the matter.

Wasn't it largely a matter of propaganda? The
newspapers, duly primed, told us that the United
States had gone mad on the song; the chorus was
printed in a good many daily and weekly journals; the
bands in restaurants and dance-halls played it; come-
dians sang it; and the mere handful of us who somehow escaped these attacks were caught by the piano-
organs and whistling errand-boys. It was what the
pseudo-scientist would call a virulent case of mass
psychology and herd instinct. So severe was the
attack that any comedian who was at a loss, and wished
to raise a laugh, had merely to say, *Yes, we have no*—
and roars of laughter drowned the remainder. Every
year—more, every half-year—sees us obsessed by
some such inane song or catchword.

It is almost entirely a matter of suggestion acting
on the sheep-like instincts of the crowd. Tell people,
by means of the daily Press, that in a few weeks' time
they will all be hailing one another with some non-
sensical expression, or singing a fatuous song, and
they are already half-way towards doing it. They

125

need only meet a few victims before succumbing completely. Such things are epidemic. But to say that the catchword is a flash of wit, and the song an inspiration, merely because they have captured everybody, is almost as foolish as to assert, during an outbreak of the disease, that measles must be a boon and a blessing on the ground that quite a lot of people are going in for it. So long as we realize that the vogue of a song is as a rule no more than a kind of measles, no harm is done. The mischief begins when people who ought to know better assert that such popularity is proof of merit.

Not long since a lecturer at University College, London, was holding forth on this point. Critics are fair game, of course, so he began with a dig at them. 'Some critics', he said, 'appeared to share a feeling of superiority, and their contempt for what was called popular music matched in many cases their hostility towards any new form or idiom.' Here we see the usual failure to distinguish between the good and bad kinds of popular music. To-day, thanks largely to the Promenade Concerts, the gramophone, wireless, and other agencies, there is an enormous amount of fine music which is popular, and no critic of standing feels contempt for it. The only objection he is likely to raise is against its over-frequent performance to the detriment of other music equally good, and equally likely to be popular. To raise objections of this kind is a part of his job, and it is a pity so reasonable an attitude is often misunderstood. But it is clear from what followed that the lecturer did not mean good popular music. He was alluding to such things as 'Yes, we have no bananas'. After pointing out that all musicians 'except perhaps a few extremely exclusive persons' (such as those sniffing critics) desired to make music more and more popular, he went on:

It would seem necessary to learn, if possible, the elements of attraction which led the populace to become infected overnight, as it were, by a certain rhythm or tune, so that, within a few hours, an arrangement of tones was being sounded by every errand-boy, and played on every street-organ.

There is no mystery, as I have tried to show above. As a proof that the vogue of a tune is usually a result of propaganda, we have the 'Bananas' example. Less often it is due to some fortuitous circumstance—e. g. even so good a tune as 'Tipperary' languished, and would have died a speedy death, but for the fact of its being sung by some of the First Expeditionary Force when starting for France.

The lecturer went on to say:

Inquiry should lead to discovery as to whether there was in popular music anything in the nature of universal elements such as were likely to win a response from minds which had received no special training in the more subtle forms of musical expression.

Why not a Royal Commission to inquire into the best methods of teaching grandmothers to suck eggs? The 'universal elements' referred to in this solemn pronouncement are tunefulness and rhythmic life, and they are found, either singly or together, in all the music that has become popular solely on its merits (that is, without any boosting or lucky topical chance), whether it be Handel's Largo or 'Johnny comes marching home', Mendelssohn's 'Spring Song' or Monckton's 'It's only a little Jappy soldier'. The public has a nose for a good tune, and when it takes violently to a bad one you may be sure that it does so because of intensive propaganda, or some homely sentimental appeal in the words, or perhaps mere chance association with some person or happening of topical interest.

§

It is a pity that as a rule the most skilful as well as the most lavish propaganda is used on behalf of bad music. On this question of public taste and propaganda here are some wise words by Chesterton, from his book on Dickens:

> I may perhaps ask leave to examine this fashionable statement—the statement that the public likes bad literature, and even likes literature because it is bad. This way of stating the thing is an error. The public does not like bad literature. The public likes a certain kind of literature, and likes that kind of literature even when it is bad better than another kind of literature even when it is good. Nor is this unreasonable; for the line between different types of literature is as real as the line between tears and laughter; and to tell people who can only get bad comedy that you have some first-class tragedy is as irrational as to offer a man who is shivering over weak, warm coffee a really superior sort of ice.

For 'literature' read 'music', and there is our case. When propaganda on behalf of good music fails the failure is generally due to the propagandists' choosing the wrong kind of good music. They should begin, and go on for a long while, with good music that happens to be rich in those 'universal elements' spoken of above, and leave the lengthy work whose beauty lies in subtlety or skilful development till later in the crusade.

The other passage from Chesterton is even more emphatic, because it deals actually with music:

> When they [the people] walk behind the brass of the Salvation Army band, instead of listening to the harmonies at Queen's Hall, it is always assumed that they prefer bad music. But it may be merely that they prefer military music, music marching down the open street, and that if Dan Godfrey's band could be smitten with salvation and lead them they would like that even better.

It all comes to this—the public usually likes what it gets; and up to very recent times, for a number of reasons (only a few of them good) the kind of music that has come its way has been mostly bad.

II

Let us look at a few tunes that have been 'boosted'
—sometimes in vain, it is good to find. I have no
scruples about giving the composer's names. They
have all enjoyed the sweets and substantial rewards
of popularity: a taste of the pillory is overdue. My
object will be to show that their alleged tunes are
almost entirely lacking in the elements that are found
in all music that has made its way by sheer merit.

Here is the refrain of a song by Ivor Novello, which
was helped (1) by being printed in certain daily newspapers (not for nothing, we may be sure); and (2) by
being sung at the Albert Hall by Dame Clara Butt:

Now, suppose that in 1914 the first Expeditionary
Force had embarked singing this refrain instead of
'Tipperary', and that it had 'caught on'—as it almost
certainly would have done in the circumstances:
would the fact prove it to be a good tune instead of the
doleful and machine-made string of notes that a
glance shows it to be? Yet we may be sure that its
popularity would have led to such comments as,
'Your highbrow classical composers can't write tunes
to capture the public as this one does.' Of course,
the answer is that classical composers have written

tunes that have been popular for generations, and will be popular for generations to come, whereas the innings of such things as 'Bubbles' and 'Yes, we have' is merely a matter of months. What is a fleeting, expensively-engineered vogue by the side of the genuine popularity enjoyed by a score of Handel's best-known tunes, Bach's so-called Air on the G string and other things, hundreds of movements and extracts from Beethoven, Chopin, Schubert, Wagner, Elgar, &c.? Our Darewskis, Ivor Novellos, and Irving Berlins don't know the difference between real popularity and a passing craze.

A Canadian journal recently published a statement of the amounts spent on popularizing song and dance 'hits' of the 'Bananas' type. The magnitude of the sums explained why even publishers of 'winners' sometimes have to put up the shutters. The article pointed out that for every success on the 'Bananas' scale, there are hundreds of failures, all of which have had bags of good hard money spent on vainly pushing them. What a showing-up it is for the compounders of so-called 'popular' songs and dances! What need is there to push the tunes of the 'high-brow classics'?

§

From Ivor Novello we pass to Herman Darewski, who has so often expressed himself publicly on the necessary constituents of popular music. The public wants tune, swing, and rhythm, he tells us, and we agree. But in his song 'The Return' he gives the public neither. Instead, he puts them off with a series of notes from which I quote (p.131) the first few groups (I refrain from the use of such words as 'melody' and 'phrases', for obvious reasons).

There are four more such groups before we reach the refrain, and every one consists almost entirely of repeated quavers, with a rhythm exactly the same as in the quotation.

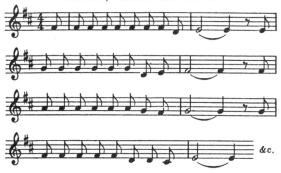

Many a song has achieved success solely by means of a catchy chorus. So generally recognized is the fact, that song-writers of this type often save themselves for the chorus, merely marking time during the song proper. So we approach Mr. Darewski's refrain with hope, almost with confidence, knowing that his hand is ever on the pulse of popular taste. But he is so sure that the public wants still more repeated quavers and a square-toed rhythm that he gives them another dose. There are six groups of notes here, two are exactly the same as the third and fourth in the quotation, and the rest are so like as to be hardly distinguishable. The refrain is ended with this graceful melodic sweep:

The second verse is an exact repetition, and by way of giving the 'tune' a good chance of soaking in, the refrain is sung twice. The accompaniment, both in harmonization and keyboard writing, is as bad as the voice part.

I may add that this is not a comic song—save unintentionally. On the contrary, it is a setting of some verses dealing with no less a topic than life beyond the grave. I do not quote the wishy-washy jingle because of the nature of the subject.

§

Now, there are some musical questions on which there can never be agreement. Because of this, we too easily yield to folk who tell us that it is impossible to label music as good or bad. It is, they say, largely a matter of taste. The fact is, of course, we can almost as easily distinguish between good and bad tunes as between good and bad eggs. Sometimes, it is true, we come across a tune that is on the border-line, just as we may meet with an egg that does nothing more than raise doubts. The only difference between the two commodities is that a tune may be good in parts, whereas a bad egg is bad all over—*pace* the hedging curate. As for the matter of taste, we know that a good many Londoners prefer an egg that has been in stock for some time: it is full-flavoured, whereas the egg that has newly come to town strikes them as tame and insipid. This does not prove that an elderly egg is good; it merely shows that as a result of being cut off from regular supplies of fresh eggs their palate has become accustomed to the bad, and has lost its taste for the good.

Would you suppose that anybody could be found to say an approving word for the song quoted above? Of course you wouldn't. Nevertheless, such a one has been found, and her testimony is set forth prominently on the cover, so that he who reads may run and buy yet more copies.

Here we will pause for a moment and consider viscountesses. Run over in your mind all the viscountesses in your circle, take any fair average specimen and ask yourself a few questions. What kind of pictures does she hang on the walls of her drawing-room? Only the best, or good copies of the best. Her

library? The shelves are full of good books, with
perhaps a few that are at all events not bad. If she
indulges in 'Heartsalve Novelettes' we may be sure
that she does not advertise the fact. Rather does she
read them privily, as the secret drinker takes his nip,
both novelette and bottle being kept out of sight. Her
furniture is good to the eye, and you may sit on it and
in all other ways use it with comfort and safety. And
so on; in all the things that really matter—cookery,
dress, and what not—you look to your viscountess to
show good sense and good taste. Only when you
come to music do you feel that anything may happen,
and that the art may be found among the what nots.

Now we get back to Mr. Darewski's song. The cover
bears the following pæan:

This beautiful song is undoubtedly an inspiration.
It touches the heart at once with its tender words and
appealing melody, breathing hope and consolation to
all humanity in its mighty declaration. . . . It is undoubtedly destined to become an anthem of joy to
many. . . .

It may or may not surprise you to hear that this
considered opinion is signed by a viscountess. There
in a nutshell is the reason why our musical life is so
chaotic. We have no standard. The lady who wrote
the above would be horrified if asked to publish her
approval of a book, or picture, or play, or fur coat, or
patent food so poor in idea and workmanship as Mr.
Darewski's song. The book would go into the waste-
paper basket, the coat back to the maker with a note
very much to the point, and the patent food would
find its way down the drain. But the song is 'beautiful', 'undoubtedly an inspiration', 'appealing melody',
'touches the heart', 'an anthem of joy', and so on.

I have taken up all this space dealing with a foolish
song and a no less foolish judgement because the time
is ripe for plain speaking on the subject. Certain of
our daily and weekly newspapers give us an abun-

dance of matter concerning the Darewskis and their output, but they can spare no more than an odd inch or two for important musical topics. In no other matter do these journals regard their readers as semi-barbarians. Their literary and theatrical columns, for example, are often first-rate. Yet the public interested in good music is almost if not quite as large as that interested in good literature and drama. So long as we musicians take no strong line in the matter, so long will our art be cold-shouldered and chivied by most of the press and made to look ridiculous by such people as Mr. Darewski and the Viscountess Moles-worth. (I see no reason for withholding the lady's name. Having, in the most public of ways, expressed her warm approval of a bad song, she cannot reason-ably complain if her judgement is discussed in an equally public manner.)

§

Here is my third example of bad music, chosen from an embarrassingly large stock of specimens. The choice is dictated in this instance by the fact of the composer having used the piece as an object-lesson in the difficult art of writing popular music. We may therefore assume that he regards it as a particularly favourable sample of his output. It occurs in a booklet by Charles Ancliffe entitled *How to write a Waltz*.

Just as there are three or four singers sharing the title of 'Queen of Song', so there are several 'Waltz Kings', and I understand Mr. Ancliffe is one of them. The Preface of his book leads the reader to expect something considerable. He tells us that 'such glori-ous examples' as the famous Waltzes of Weber, Tchaikovsky, Sibelius, &c., 'illustrate the claims of the waltz to be regarded seriously, even by highbrows' (why 'even'? Does Mr. Ancliffe think that only Charing Cross Road has an ear for the 'Invitation', the 'Valse des fleures', &c.?), and goes on to speak reproachfully of 'the plagiarism and borrowing that is so rampant to-day'. He then proceeds to take the aspirant through his own *Southern Nights*, explaining the construction, and drawing attention to various beauties on the way. As *Southern Nights* lacks any sort of freshness in matter or manner, it is amusing to read such dicta as the following:

Originality in melody, harmony, construction, or design, makes for lasting quality. In the ephemeral type known as the vocal waltz, which usually dies in a few months, these qualities are conspicuous by their absence. The paucity of invention and general puerility of both words and music condemn them to early oblivion, and it is devoutly to be hoped that a return to the legitimately musicianly waltz may be not far distant.

There is truth in Mr. Ancliffe's remark that 'melodies that live are generally the product of a mood of exaltation', and as to the importance of the opening theme being 'good, strong, arresting . . . original, and striking'. If he had left it at that all would have been well, but he goes on to quote the opening theme of his own waltz, and we look in vain for the qualities on which he rightly insists:

There is scarcely a bar here that is not weak in melody, harmony, rhythm, or laying-out. One might give a helpful lesson in composition based on its examples of what to avoid.

I pass on to the discussion of the Coda:

Here again [says Mr. Ancliffe] sincerity is our watchword. A mere fading away, or a few reiterated chords, because there is nothing more to say, will not do at all. . . . We must see to it that the last heard of our waltz is worth remembering. . . . The *Coda* is to be regarded as the coping-stone . . . and it must not be scamped or treated lightly . . . it must heighten the effect of what has gone before, not obliterate it. This latter is what a hastily-written *Coda* will do.

With all this insistence on originality, invention, sincerity, coping-stones, &c., in mind, we turn with interest to see what Mr. Ancliffe does by way of Coda to *Southern Nights*—presumably his best work (I repeat), seeing that he takes it as the model for his lesson. Here is the Coda:

If you haven't heard the harmonic basis of bars 1–6 many a time and oft at the hands and feet of tenth-rate organists you have been luckier than I. The puerility of this coping-stone is not excused by the fact that, melodically, it is derived from themes used earlier in the work. It has to be judged as a coping-stone, pure and simple, and a mighty poor specimen it is.

I spend all this space on such a subject because the time is come for a clearing up of some of these questions concerning popular music. The public needs to be shown that popular music may be good or bad, just as classical music may be good or bad—though it has taken some musicians a long while to grasp the latter fact. Hitherto, we have been too complacent— lazy is the truer word—and as a result there is a lot of muddled thinking on the part of the public. Fine work is being done in the way of bringing great music to the ear of the crowd, but we shall achieve only a lop-sided result so long as that ear is so persistently assailed by bad popular music. Wouldn't it be starting at the right end if we worked rather on the lines suggested in the Chesterton quotation, and gave the public good examples of the kind of music it wants, rather than trying (often at great financial risk) to get its members to appreciate good music of a type that is so far new to most of them, and therefore unwanted? Anyway, we must no longer leave a clear field to shoddy. And we must let the shoddy merchant see that he can't go on turning out 'best sellers' of the type quoted above, and at the same time expect to be regarded as a musician. He is ready enough to throw 'highbrow' at all who see through his flimsy pretensions. If the possession of a brow of the type peculiar to the simian species gives him satisfaction, he is welcome to it. But if he parades a false front on occasion, he mustn't expect to deceive the real high- brows—who are not at all ashamed of a decent frontal development and all that it connotes.

ART: ARISTOCRATIC OR POPULAR?

EFFORTS on behalf of the popularization of good music are now so extensive and so powerfully sponsored that we are apt to overlook some obvious dangers to the art itself; and those who are aware of them are loth to speak their mind for fear of being misunderstood.

For example, not long ago a few of us protested against the practice of asking the audience at children's concerts to sing, to nonsense rhymes, themes from classical works. We were called wet blankets, spoilsports, pedants, and other hard names; and were accused of trying to 'crab' the efforts of those engaged in spreading the love of good music. Of course, we were doing nothing of the sort. Our contention was that people of all ages could be brought to realize the beauty of a work without recourse to methods which tended to cheapen it. The association of a fine theme with anything ludicrous is a hindrance rather than a help. The association may be set up in a moment or two, and may rouse laughter, but it is liable to stick for years. For example, there are certain of Bach's themes that I can never hear without recalling some jingles used at a children's concert a few years ago. It is so easy to vocalize or merely hum a theme that there is no excuse for saddling it, and us, with a piece of nonsense that may become an obsession.

I mention this as an example of the lack of thought that too often goes with propagandist enthusiasm; and the subject has been brought to mind by a very striking article entitled 'For the People', by Alexander Fried, in *Modern Music*, an American quarterly. In a nutshell, Mr. Fried's view is that the best music—indeed, good music generally—is not for the crowd; and that efforts to make it so will take the bloom off the music itself.

139

This is a proposition that will find little favour among musicians; but even those of us who refuse to accept it will profit by thinking a little on Mr. Fried's arguments. No doubt the conditions in America differ from those in this country. Propaganda, whether aesthetic or ethical, is much less lavish on this side of the Atlantic, mainly because we are still a nation of individualists. Instinctively we feel that, having provided opportunities for culture, we have no call to do much more. In America they not only lead the horse to the water (which is more than we do here, as a rule; we merely stick up signposts, 'To the water; take it or leave it!'); they actually try to make the animal drink.

A certain allowance must therefore be made for Mr. Fried's point of view; but even when that is done, his main contention is worth consideration.

He begins by saying that an essential part of the American democratic creed is 'a belief in the possibility of completely educating the masses'. In the United States to-day there is 'an unprecedented propaganda for the popularization of serious music'. The enthusiast points with pride to such evidences of success as a good audience at a 'musical appreciation' concert, the formation of a new musical club, the endowment of another orchestra, &c. But the flushed triumphant propagandist fails to realize that these things have to be estimated in their relation to other phenomena in the social system of to-day. Says Mr. Fried:

> In all innocence he forgets that in our present era of wealth and well-being every kind of showmanship is prospering as never before. To parallel the increase in the symphony clientèle, there are statistics of the stunning advance in popularity of the movies, comic strips, football, record air flights, and a thousand other activities directly or indirectly attracting the public interest. If the growing number of endowed orchestras

signifies important cultural progress in the life of the nation, what does it mean that thirty or forty million Americans passionately concern themselves in a prize fight that a few years ago would have touched hardly a tenth that many?

This is a truth that applies to practically every civilized country. Where twenty-five years ago a few people went almost daily to some kind of show, a hundred go to-day. Before we throw up our hats over large attendances at concerts, let us count those at the cinema, the dance hall, and a score of other places of amusement.

However, Mr. Fried is not so greatly concerned over the chance that the propaganda may fail. (Indeed, he seems almost to *fear* that ultimately it may succeed!) The menace is, rather,

. . . the possible bad influence of the propaganda, as it is carried out, on the art itself. It has not harmed poetry, painting, or sculpture to affect only a tiny minority of each generation. But we have seen what the will of the masses has done to such an institution as our newspapers; the more popular they are, the worse they are.

So large a proportion of the public, of all classes and degrees of culture, are regular patrons of the cinema that Mr. Fried is justified in taking it as a guide. He contends that cinema art is what it is—crude, banal, and obvious—because the public demands that kind of art; only a minute percentage of genuinely artistic films pay their way. And he quotes a cinema authority as saying: 'To me the fact that a motion picture is a popular and financial success is a perfect indication that it is, in an artistic sense, a bad picture'.

This statement [says Mr. Fried] describes the public taste more than it does the cinema. It includes, besides, disconcerting implications of the potential relations between serious music and the masses at whom hopeful educators aim their efforts to make operatic, symphonic, and chamber music a persuasive and popular art.

Mr. Fried takes too little account, I think, of the deplorable lack of taste—and even of ordinary educa-. tion—shown by the average film producer. Against his theory that the demand for vulgarity has created the supply we may set the adage that 'the appetite grows by what it feeds on'. Until a few years ago the gramophone was pretty much what the cinema still is, so far as the character and quality of its output were concerned. A more courageous and enlightened policy has shown that there is a very large public for records of fine music. It is reasonable to suppose that a similar policy in connexion with the cinema would produce a corresponding result. What would the taste of our wireless public be like if the B.B.C. were composed of Hollywood film producers?

§

Mr. Fried is on firmer ground when he refuses to be enthusiastic concerning the use of good music in picture theatres:

In the familiarly touted popularization of serious music at the bigger movie theatres, the thesis of the intrinsic exclusiveness of fine art is again strongly supported. Since the first fad of the symphony orchestra, many of the feature houses have fallen back on jazz and semi-jazz musical combinations. In the few theatres where 'good music' has been retained, sad as the truth may be, the will of the public has an evil effect on performance. The movie programme is ridiculously limited to the most blatant numbers in the symphony repertory, and even the 'Marche Slave' and the 'Spanish Caprice' are commonly cut and re-orchestrated to flavour them to popular taste.

It is, of course, largely a matter of atmosphere and environment:

Beyond everything, there is a spirit in ordinary movie interpretation thoroughly alien to genuine musical sense. Cheap exaggeration of every fundamental musical effect is only part of the disfigurement. It is beyond conception that a movie audience should listen in patience to a slow movement, an extended passage of modestly beautiful phrasing, a true cantilena. I have never heard an unqualifiedly conscientious reading of first-rate music in a popular theatre. It does not 'go over'.

Nor must we be in a hurry to blame the picture-theatre musician:

Much as the movie musical director may regret what he does, he knows the mass public. His inevitable business is to satisfy it with what it understands to be entertainment. He is aware that the populace has not the mental poise and penetration to sit through fine music well performed, to sense the effectiveness of intricate and ingenious composition, to be moved by the beauty of pure music. Therefore he cuts scores, splices hideously conflicting material, improvises trite jazzifications, arranges his readings by the watch, accompanies abstract music with a thousand irrelevant and obvious effects of light and dancing.

Mr. Fried holds that the American general musical public is not appreciably less equipped with musical taste than other publics are—or even have been. He contends (rightly) that much of the popular appeal of Liszt, for example, had little to do with music. Italy rejoices in 'Il Trovatore', and has little ear for symphonic music:

In the best days of music in Germany, the love of it was as widespread as it probably will be anywhere. Two reasons account for this: the tremendous prestige of support from the upper classes and the lack of competing entertainers.

Again, music has, in the past, often gained because of its association with 'powerful public loyalties and observances, such as religion and nationalism':

Nowadays the sacred association has declined, and the nationalistic bond is feeble, despite all efforts to strengthen it. It is left to music to become popular

143

of itself. In our present society and culture, the art must automatically be harmed in proportion as popularization is successful. To compete in catching skilfully-sought public interest, music must posture and gesticulate in antics such as those which make our newspapers and movies abominable. Some branches of the art, it is true, have greater potential showmanship than others. The mere co-operation of a hundred musicians in an orchestra is sufficiently spectacular to interest a fairly large group of our population—perhaps as much as five per cent. Opera, which is palpably brilliant and showy, is always most esteemed for its least admirable qualities.

There is much in this. In fact, I am of opinion that children's concerts begin at the wrong end by concentrating on the orchestra. The extra-musical attractions are so powerful that a youngster who gets his first liking for music through the orchestra is pretty sure to complain that mere pianoforte, chamber, or vocal music is dull. Is this a desirable state of things?

Mr. Fried sums up in favour of the old view that music is an aristocratic art. It must cater for the few, if it is to remain an art. The moment it begins to draw the crowd it is in danger of ceasing to be an art and becoming a mere show:

There is no possibility of making a string quartet appeal to the masses if it is satisfied to embellish its art and reputation simply with the aesthetic virtues of good chamber music. By playing beautiful works beautifully the small ensemble can gather only a small clientèle. It ought to be satisfied with that and its art. No doubt the audience would increase, for a moment, if the first violinist were to kill his wife, swim the English Channel, or marry the Queen of Rumania, but music cannot make the first page consistently without contamination.

And he ends on a note of dejection:

Supreme music cannot, any more than Keats, commune with the heart of the multitude, any more than

Santayana can speak to its mind. Intelligence and specialised sensibility are not distributed with the voting privilege.

§

The weakness of Mr. Fried's argument as a whole is due to its being based on the assumption that good music (or as he apparently prefers to call it, serious music) is an easily classifiable unit, instead of an immense and very diverse collection. The popularity of the best-selling fox-trot of to-day is as nothing beside the popularity of a great mass of good music. The fox-trot is here to-day and gone to-morrow, whereas hundreds of songs and pieces by the great composers, from Handel and Bach onwards, have been a stand-by to ordinary folk for generations.

The qualities that have won them this enduring popularity are usually easy to determine. It would be difficult to name an example that has neither a good tune nor a vital rhythm. On the other hand, it would be as hard to find one that owes its popularity to its harmony alone. Here surely is a guide to propagandists. I have often been amazed at the type of music chosen for missionary purposes. There is plenty of good music, of all periods, that is immediately attractive, and the propagandist should always go to this field for his examples. All art falls roughly into two divisions, one for popular consumption, the other for the specialist; and it is snobbery to hold that the latter is necessarily superior. As often as not, the difference is one of kind rather than of quality.

The audience that is to be converted may never have a chance of a second hearing, still less a third and fourth; and it is absurd to give it music that reveals its beauty only after long acquaintance. Even here, however, we must distinguish between music that is at first a sealed book, and that which, though no less serious and complex, makes a good part of its effect at once. For example, many of the quick Fugues in the 'Forty-eight' attract immediately by reason of their rhythmic animation and continuity. Mr. Robert Blatchford recently wrote an article describing his sudden conversion to Bach. He didn't know one end of a fugue from another, so to speak; yet the healthy energy of the 'Forty-eight' had a tonic effect on him, and he is now a confirmed fugueite, though still ignorant of music generally. I would back (say) the C sharp major in Book I, or the rattling two-voiced Fugue in E minor, against an average classical slow movement, so far as making an instant appeal to an average untrained hearer is concerned. Yet I have heard well-meaning 'appreciationists' dosing a crowd with a whole string of works almost devoid of melodic or rhythmic appeal—first movements that consisted largely of passage-work and development of the type that the generation of to-day has no ears for; Adagios that were practically static, standing mostly on one leg, and gently pawing the air or meditating with the other; and Finales that did just the same as the first movement, with the saving grace of being a bit quicker over the job.

§

All music chosen for propaganda use should be tuneful and rhythmic—especially rhythmic. These qualities are far more important than simplicity. In fact, simplicity often calls for a good deal of sophistication in the listener, whereas when both tunefulness and rhythm are present in abundance, they can carry on their back almost any amount of complexity.

Thus, few untutored listeners can be deaf to the splendours of the 'Mastersingers' Overture; and little is gained (something may even be lost) by telling them that it is a masterpiece of polyphony, and that they will hear Wagner using three themes at once if they listen very hard, with an ear for each theme. Let them begin by enjoying it as a bit of splendid sound, shot with good tunes, and full of lively rhythms.

And, talking of polyphony, I suggest we should be cautious in administering doses of old madrigals. Such things are far more interesting to the singer than to the hearer. This is no defect, of course; they were written, like chamber music (which they are, in a sense), for doers rather than hearers.

Save as single numbers, and carefully chosen, they should be reserved for audiences of specialists, such as the regular patrons of a madrigal choir. Their indiscriminate choice as test-pieces for competition festival use (especially for village and small town choirs) is risky. They call for a special palate and a special technique, and until both are acquired by means of demonstration and by a very carefully graded choice, choirs and their supporters are likely to revolt. Their words, too, are often a stumbling-block. Diction, imagery, and topics alike rouse no sympathy in the average choralist. How should they? Are there many enthusiastic readers of the madrigal poems, even in literary circles? If not, need we be surprised that the average singer gets bored after a few months' invocation of Thyrsis, Chloris, and Amaryllis, with three times three for fair Oriana by way of Coda? A good modern part-song, with words by such writers as Bridges, de la Mare, Masefield, Noyes, &c., is more attractive fare—and often better music, I am bold to say.

Finally, the only way to fight lively bad music is to give the crowd plenty of lively good music. This is so obvious that I hesitate to set it down. Yet over and over again chances are missed by a failure to grasp the importance of this elementary manœuvre. Thus, if you want to prove that an old dance can stand up against a fox-trot (and even drive it off the floor), you will hardly do it with a faded Strauss waltz or a stately pavane. Take a lively jig, or rigaudon, or a graceful gavotte. For purely listening purposes (which is the point under consideration) hasn't old Boccherini's Minuet in A, for example, outlived thousands of fox-trots during the past ten years?

Let Mr. Fried cheer up. Hardly one of the great composers failed to write a good deal of music that appeals to all alike, as do bread, water, beer, onions, and a hundred other of the great simple things of life. Give the crowd these—the dances of Bach, the tunes of Handel, the Overtures of Weber, and a host of other operatic composers, the 'Rakoczy' March, the 'Songs without Words' (I hear a refined shudder), the C sharp minor Prelude (a cultured groan: but why? I wish all modern pianoforte music were as good), Chopin's Polonaise in A and a dozen of his Waltzes and Nocturnes, the 'Pomp and Circumstance' Marches, and so on. The list is almost endless.

There is no need to moan over the taste of people who like these things—as millions certainly do. They have the root of the matter in them, and all that is left for the propagandist to do is to widen their horizon by giving them plenty of good music of the same readily enjoyable type, with a judicious mixture of things that call for a little more taking-in. Even if the man in the street stops at such pieces as those mentioned above, he will be far from being a Philistine. When his taste in books, plays, and picture-shows is as good, an æsthetic revolution will have taken place.

JINGLE AT THE BALLET
(1921)

SHORTAGE of space compels me to reduce language to
bare bones, à la Alfred Jingle. Such meagre doings
appropriate—brings writer into line with ultra-modern
composer: elimination of unessential. (Blessed words
like Mespot—but observe with pain that, despite
paring-down, modern composer takes long while
deliver goods; should carry elimination farther—be
ruthless. Why stop at unessential?)

Stravinsky still storm-centre in critical circles.
Leave fighting to advance-guard of disputants—one
says bubble burst—other equally sure no bubble:
epoch-making music. Truth most likely between two.
Heard 'Sacre du Printemps' as symphony twice—
thrills at times—nary a thrill at good many others—
unequal work, very. But thrills unusually potent—
made me wish hear work again and again—especially
if second part drastically cut. Had no doubt, though,
that performance as ballet would strengthen weak
spots. Expected Russians provide right choregraphy
—brutal and elemental—notable powers that way.
But subject beat them. Primitive methods of hailing
Spring far from idyllic—quite reverse—disgraceful
goings on—but all in good faith—no harm meant—
simple folk—ages dark—very. Fit subject for folk-
lore societies, but as for stage representation—Tut!
Still one might skirt round border-line picturesquely.
But early Russians, as represented by late ones at
theatre, dull dogs. When in Spring *their* fancy lightly
turned to thoughts of pairing off, no gusto—no 'once-
aboard-the-lugger' style—lots of tame calisthenics—
kind of thing Lieutenant Müller would have us do
a-mornings—knees bend—rise on toes—reach right
arm round left shoulder and count vertebrae—if you
can; repeat with left arm—again if you can—fatigu-

ing even for lissom Russians—boring for audience—
very. Amorous flights hardly more entertaining.
Each sad young man selects no less melancholy
damsel—hauls her on shoulder (regretfully, as if
would have preferred sister)—carries her across stage
—gently dumps her down—begins fresh batch of
Müllerisms. Assembled damsels (now on verge of
tears) fall to round games of simple and depressing
character. Sokolova, who should do nothing but flit
and float, so far wasted. Stationary—Patience on
monument—holding jaw (literally)—deep in thought
—or tense with toothache. In last few minutes of
ballet woke up—released jaw—brought house down
with frenzied solo dance—saved ballet from utter
failure—like top note at end of poor song: fetches
'em, but poor song all the same. Ditto ballet.
Tumultuous applause from one section of audience—
rich and eloquent silence from another—hisses from
yet another. Ayes apparently had it—but ballet given
only three times, then withdrawn—so noes right after
all. Personally sorry show poor—had hoped and
expected conversion; wished could join in convulsive
transports of rapt critic, Henry Leigh, who improvised
ballet on his own in stalls—stout work with arms and
hands—costly cane (apparently knobbed with gold of
Ophir) projecting at dangerous angle—stout gentleman leaving in hurry nearly impaled himself; fortunately dress shirt superstarched—unexpected breast-
plate—ferrule glanced off—all well—lucky escape—
very.

§

Had no intention of discussing ballets in particular.
Began with idea of trying to say how ballet in general
strikes plain man such as writer. First, observe ballet
audiences most uncritical mob. Hysterical applause—
bouquets—laurel wreaths—no matter whether good
or bad work on stage. Believe if disguised myself as

Woizikovsky (though figure perhaps obstacle) and capered uncouthly while orchestra tuned up would receive ovation. Henry Leigh and other advanced pioneers would say choregraphy of right kind, free from hint of grace of rhythm, and music happily devoid of emotion and poetic or literary suggestion—polyphony of rhythm and tonal values juxtaposed all over the shop. Less advanced spectators would beat hands together—cry 'bravo!'—lest they should appear behind times—better be dead than out of date at the Russian ballet. Same uncritical attitude makes them swallow all silly affectations and conventions. A form much overrated—plain man finds choregraphy often mere distraction when music is good. As for miming, absence of spoken word involves exaggerated facial expression as in 'cinema'. Moreover, too little real dancing. Plain man wants more things like the miller's dance in 'Three-Cornered Hat'. Thinks, too, that toe dancing is overdone. Admits its difficulty—tried it himself one morning waiting for bath—humiliating failure—should have begun when many years younger and slimmer—not years slimmer, of course, but inches —or feet. Anyway, difficulty does not justify these Russians over-doing it—effect that of short stilts—stilt-walking ugly—word 'stilted' just fits case. Plain man wonders, too, why stage must be always so dusty —dancers with exquisite shoes—sometimes no less exquisite bare feet—sight for sore eyes till they show soles—black with grime—why? Stage should be like deck of ship—one can eat dinner off it—yet one never does, somehow. If dust necessary for grip use pink dust—match feet and look well on shoes. No doubt plain man Philistine and all behind times—plain man always is. Not a bit ashamed of it.

Still, spent some enjoyable hours at ballet. Wish more were as good as 'Petrouchka'. Odd, when think of it—most poignant and human of modern ballets concerned chiefly with puppets, while in some others

humans are no more convincing than animated lay
figures. Conducting of Ansermet one of chief sources
of pleasure—few things more picturesque than sil-
houette against lighted stage. Eloquent hands—
captivating beard when seen in profile—not mere
hairy extra but real feature—something to swear by,
like Beard of Prophet—active and eloquent, too—
could have sworn Ansermet produced fine *sforzando*
with it one night. Late-comers in stalls silhouetted
less flatteringly. Surprising number of profiles unable survive ordeal—too much nose (children of
Shem)—not enough chin (decadent youth)—too
much chin—several too many in fact (overfed boor-
jwaw)—heads wrong shape—forehead in unusual
place—somehow got round behind—skull like plateau
with small concavity (bath for canary)—or high and
dome-like (excellent for perch after bath).

§

Returning to Ballet, must give thanks for valuable
health tip. Writer getting on in years—worried about
equator—steadily increasing despite Spartan diet.
Week ago started doing daily extracts from 'Sacre du
Printemps'—twenty minutes on rising—unaccom-
panied of course, and no damsel around—knees bend
—rise on toes—reach right arm round left shoulder
and almost count vertebrae—repeat with left arm—
breath in short pants—but marked improvement in
figure already. By the time can call it 'Sacre de
l'Automne' hope to be once more agile stripling of
dear dead days beyond recall.

PS.—Restaurant music long since a noisy bore—
now become positive obstacle to busy man's taking
nourishment. Hungry and hurried last night—unusual experience (the former, that is) tottered faint-
ing from Ballet into ever-open door of popular
restaurant—sank into seat—huge place—got up
regardless—dreamt-I-dwelt-in-marble-halls kind of

thing. Secured attention of neat-handed Phyllis—
gave modest order befitting humble journalist. Crash
from orchestra at far end of hall about a furlong away
—burly baritone burst into ballad—761 diners ceased
stoking—same number of forks suspended between
plate and mouth, each bearing due portion of victuals
—baritone going strong—alien—throat of brass—
forehead of ditto—lungs of leather; glad there is a
furlong between us. Meanwhile pangs of hunger
developing rapidly—that sinking feeling—beckon
neat-handed Phyllis. 'Is food coming?' Phyllis very
sorry and all that—cannot fetch food till song over—
instructions—much as place is worth. Venture to
explain—came for food, not for concert. Have no use
for concert just now, but immediate and pressing
need of food. Point of view evidently new to Phyllis—
nonplussed—calls superior officer; another alien.
'Ver' sorry! No can do; streekt orders—silence while
ze museek; she not long now—near feenish.' In
support of plea, indicated suspended forks (only 760
now, one impatient client silently wolfing under cover
of evening paper). Nothing for it but to wait. When
song ended at long last forks got busy again, and Phyllis
procured food. Managed to bolt it—then bolted
myself just as Leather-lungs got on hind legs for
another song. Shall avoid restaurant in future. Don't
like this application of old saw, 'No song, no supper.'
Good deal to be said for its inversion though. Dreamt
last night was at vocal recital—consulted programme
and waited for first song. Attendant approached
respectfully—Sorry to keep me waiting, but rule of
management, 'No supper, no song.' Could recom-
mend cutlet. Would I kindly wait for song till I have
eaten? Would I? Would I *not*? Cutlet delicious—
just decided, after all, much to be said in favour of
encores, when woke up.

153

'ON PAPER'

THE typewriter has long since sounded the doom of penmanship. Will the efforts to construct a music-typewriting machine bear fruit, and do the same for music copying? A good many years ago a Dickens enthusiast in his mid-'teens stood before the manuscripts of some of the novelist's books preserved in the Forster Bequest at the South Kensington Museum. No matter how many more years he may have left to him, he will never forget the emotion with which he gazed and gazed at those close-written pages. To read of the falling-out of Mrs. Gamp and Miss Prig—for the Chuzzlewit MS. lay open at that moving page—in the brisk hand of Dickens himself, with a word altered here and there, was to become a kind of co-creator. The young enthusiast approved the scratchings-out and the writings-in, and left a more devoted Dickensian than he went in. I know, for I was that youth.

And now, thanks to the cunning of photographer and printer, I can enjoy much the same experience with Bach, Mozart, and Beethoven. Before me lie facsimiles of a Bach Cantata, a Mozart Trio, and a Beethoven Sonata—the C minor, Op. 111. They are the last word in faithful reproduction. Everything is there, from the catastrophic blot down to the faintest discoloration of the paper. And as we can see Dickens at work in those bulky MS. books at South Kensington, so we may see the composers in these facsimiles.[1]

§

Bach must always have been more or less in a hurry. How else could he have done so much, even in his long life? Like the rest of us, however, he starts on a job with neatness. 'This shall really be a clean and tidy copy,' he seems to say, and for the opening page

[1] Drei Masken Verlag, Munich.

154

all goes well. But at the first turnover things are against him. For a start, the little contraption with which he rules his music lines—probably a wheel arrangement of the kind still used by frugal souls—ruins three staves by allowing the ink (apparently a solution of the Day & Martin of the period) to run, so that two lines join forces, and what ought to be a space becomes a broad band of solid black. Hopeless to attempt any notes there, so two staves are left blank, and a third impatiently crossed through. Gone already is the hope of a model manuscript! Half-way down the next page Bach wants to make a correction. Erase? No time; besides, as well be hanged for a sheep as for a lamb, so across the passage goes the side of his little finger, and over the pale smear the new notes are written. For the rest of this chorus nothing matters beyond getting the notes down, so there are passages that make one giddy to look at. But he starts the next number—an Aria—with neatness and some signs of leisure, only to become, a page later, hasty and barely legible. The writing is bold. Groups of semiquavers are braced together by thick strokes which leave so many hollow squares and projecting ends of stems that one could well play a game of noughts and crosses with the result. Indications as to performance are few—just enough phrasing and bowing marks to put an intelligent performer on the right tack; why waste time by adding more? Besides, space is precious. If you and I had to rule our own manuscript paper we should do as Bach did—get as many staves as possible on a page, with the result that there is little room left for anything beyond the bare notes. One wonders what the old man would say could he see a modern score, bristling with expression marks (ninety per cent. of them unnecessary) and larded with flowers of speech in half a dozen tongues, from *crescendo molto al fortissimo* to 'Louden, lots'. I can see him waving such a score away, with a hasty,

'Why so many marks? Either the composer daren't trust his own music, or he has a poor opinion of his performers.' In fact, it is not an overstatement to say that a fool-proof edition always has a fool at one end or the other—sometimes at both.

§

After the bold and hurried manuscript of Bach, that of Mozart seems beautifully clear. Like Bach, he had no time to waste, but he was luckier in his tools—a properly printed manuscript-book, a slightly better brand of blacking, and a pen that allowed of thinner note-stems and neater work with rests, dots, and slurs. There are very few alterations. One could play from most of the copy with little inconvenience. The Finale is of special interest. All goes well for a page and a half, at which point Mozart breaks off at a half-close on the dominant. Then he appears to have left the work for awhile. Anyhow, when he does take it up again he starts with a new pen. But what avails a new pen if the ideas dry up? A few bars farther on the movement peters out with the right hand of the pianoforte part, and the rest of the page is blank. 'This won't go,' he says, 'I may as well cut my losses and make a fresh start'—which he does on the following page with entirely new material, and thereafter the Finale flows as we expect it to flow from Mozart. The new pen gets worn soft towards the end, and appears to have hard work in keeping up with the composer's invention. But despite the growing haste, neatness is never lost. The whole thing is somehow just what we expect from Mozart.

In the Beethoven copy we have a surprise. The theatrical view of Beethoven as a rugged, titanic figure dies so hard that one has a bit of a shock on seeing this manuscript. It is hopelessly untidy and sketchy from start to finish, the notes slope wildly from left to right, and corrections are often indecipherable—so much so that Beethoven has to write over the confused scratches the names of the notes. A sight-reader who could make out the Arietta, with its pages of demisemiquavers and ledger lines, would be a champion. Character? Well, if the writer of this manuscript were a woman, we should say at once 'here is a Cat of the first order, and then some'.

§

One lays these engrossing facsimiles aside feeling that the general adoption of a music typewriter will be a boon to the engraver, and perhaps to the composer, but that it will cheat posterity of some human documents. Who, fifty years hence, will give a fig to see the typescript of a Galsworthy novel or an Elgar symphony?

On the whole, however, it seems likely that the music typewriter, however soon it may come, will be too late to be of much use. A machine of the kind might be able to deal with the straightforward music of a Beethoven, but how would it fare with the complications of a Schönberg? Or even of the normal modern composer?

Just as the resources of the pen itself are highly tried by the flights of our more extreme composers, so even the ten fingers multiplied by the sustaining pedal do not always suffice the pianoforte writer. I have before me a work recently published in America —Charles E. Ives's second Sonata entitled *Concord, Mass., 1840–60*. It opens with, and is interspersed by, pages of reading matter—windy transcendentalism for the most part. Its four movements are entitled 'Emerson', Hawthorne', 'The Alcotts', and 'Thoreau', so it is programme music, the scheme of which is plain to most English people who have a fair acquaintance with American literature. Like most programme music, of course, it conveys nothing of its meaning without the labels. However, I do not propose to go

into that side of the Sonata. I mention it here because
it is a striking example of the modern tendency to
write music whose effect very largely remains on
paper. It is probably one of the most difficult pianoforte works ever written, and a prolonged and anxious
search for a few gleams of beauty or genuine simplicity has drawn blank. I resist the temptation to
quote some of the uglier and more hopelessly difficult
passages, and confine myself to three, wherein the
composer finds the ten fingers inadequate. On page
21 we have a good many bars of this sort of thing:

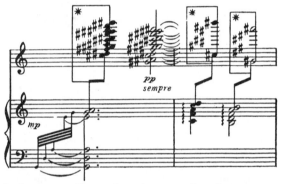

A footnote tells us that these stacks of notes are
played 'by using a strip of board 14¾ in. long, and
heavy enough to press the keys down without striking'. Whether the player or an assistant is to apply
this piece of timber is not stated, but I do not see how
the player is to manage it. As a rule the wood is placed
on the black keys only, but on one occasion it comes
down good and hard on sixteen white ones (p. 159).

Of what use is this puerile device? I can hear
some one ask, 'Why use wood? What is the matter
with a good leg-of-mutton fist?' Mr. Ives gives the
answer. 'Nothing,' he says, in effect; 'the fist is all
right'; and sure enough, on pages 40 and 41 he gives

158

it an innings. He begins by writing bunches of semi-quavers for the right hand against a running bass,

telling the player that the bunches are best managed by 'using the palm of the hand or the clenched fist'. A couple of lines later he calls on both fists, thus:

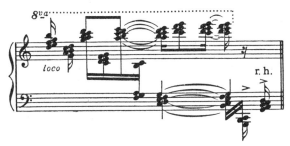

The sustaining pedal is kept down while about fifty of these stout blows are struck, and the passage is marked *fff*. Leaving the reader to supply the necessary comments on this music, I add that, the seventy pages of the Sonata being ended, the composer tacks on about three thousand words of epilogue of which the following is a sample:

Beauty, in its common conception, has nothing to do with it [substance], unless it be granted that its outward aspect, or the expression between sensuous beauty and spiritual beauty, can be always and distinctly known, which it cannot, as the art of music is still in its infancy. However, it cannot justly be said that anything that has to do with art has nothing to do with beauty in any degree—that is, whether beauty is there or not, it has something to do with it. A casual idea of it, a kind of first necessary-physical impression, was what we had in mind . . . we like the beautiful and don't like the ugly; therefore, what we like is beautiful and what we don't like is ugly—and hence we are glad the beautiful is not ugly, for if it were we would like something we don't like.

This sort of thing seems oddly familiar. Where have I met with it before? I take down *Martin Chuzzlewit*, and find another great American thinker talking in pretty much the same style. Miss Codger, you will (or should) remember, on being presented to Mr. Elijah Pogram by Mrs. Hominy, said promptly:

To be presented to a Pogram by a Hominy, indeed, a thrilling moment is it in its impressiveness on what we call our feelings. But why we call them so, or why impressed they are, or if impressed they are at all, or if at all we are, or if there really is, oh gasping one! a Pogram or a Hominy, or any active principle to which we give those titles, is a topic, Spirit searching, light abandoned, much too vast to enter on, at this unlooked-for crisis.

You observe Mr. Ives's opinion that music is at present in its infancy. He develops the idea elsewhere, speaking hopefully of the time 'when the school children will whistle popular tunes in quarter-tones, when the diatonic scale will be as obsolete as the pentatonic is now'. May I *not* be there to hear! And if this Sonata is a specimen of music in its infancy, what will Mr. Ives produce when he has a really grown-up art to play with?

§

Something was said above about the modern over-use of expression marks. Undoubtedly they are losing their point through being over-done. 'When everyone is somebodee, then no-one's anybody'; and when a composer is at us all the time with fussy directions he soon leaves us indifferent. Bach used one mark where a composer to-day uses a hundred, yet, given a performer of good average ability, the result is the same. In fact, the mark in music has depreciated. With us, a big bagful goes a mighty little way, whereas Bach made a few suffice for a lengthy work.

One of the most absurd examples of overmarked music lies before me in the shape of a set of nine pieces for pianoforte, called *A Bermuda Suite*, by Robert Huntington Terry. Mr. Terry is nothing if not explicit. It is not enough to mark the close of a piece *rall.* or *morendo*. He must needs write, *retard here softly and holding back reluctantly*. And an *8va* mark may be misunderstood, so he adds *Play this an octave higher*. In the piece called 'Crystal Cave' he spreads himself, and for a page and a half keeps up a running directorial comment placed between the staves in such a way that I found myself beginning to sing it:

A sound of distant bells and tones of an organ as suggested by huge stalactites. *ff*. The subterranean lake impresses one of its marvellous beauty, and one hears the dripping of water from the stalactites. Mark the theme very broadly; but the staccato notes without regarding the time; here and there, increasing in tone, then decrease again.

Despite the shaky English, this seems to make things clear, doesn't it? But the composer's motto is 'Safety first', so he adds a footnote:

The notes above the theme must be played very lightly and softly, *rubato* time, to represent water dripping into a lake, almost suggesting a perfect melody, not in strict time.

Not a doubt of it; Mr. Terry wants those little notes at the top to be played quietly and in free time like little drops of water falling from the whatnots. I may add that the theme for which such breadth is demanded is a poor affair of less interest than a third-rate hymn-tune. There is nothing surprising in this. Good wine needs no bush, and fine music can dispense with trimmings. If a theme has character of any kind we shall be aware of it.

§

Finally, has it ever struck you that our present system of notation, full of absurdities though it be, can and does present us with pages that are a real joy to the eye as well as to the ear? This is especially the case when a gracefully undulating figure is used persistently. Some of the Preludes in the '48' are delightful to look at, e.g. the C major and C sharp major in Book I, and the C sharp major in Book II. Take up almost any volume of Chopin and you will find pages of beautiful design, e.g. the F sharp minor Prelude, the spreading figure in the L.-H. part of the B flat Prelude, the Berceuse (when not too closely engraved), the F major and C minor Studies, &c. And even when there is no regular pattern, the delicate arabesques in little notes add a fine and dainty touch. Most of the scintillating decorative passages in Tchaikovsky's orchestral scores look as pleasing as they sound. The *Nutcracker* Suite is specially good: look at the Arab and Chinese dances, the Dragon-fly, and (above all) the middle section of the Mirlitons dance. There is a section of Beethoven's ninth Symphony that always calls for a second glance —the last twenty bars of the first movement, where the octave leaps of the strings and the rhythmic figure of the wind make a handsome pattern.

And we may forgive Stravinsky many of his sounds for this pretty design in crotchets, from the 'Danse du Diable' in *L'Histoire du Soldat*:

The prize, however, must go to the following, kindly brought to my notice by Mr. Sydney Grew. It is from a Foxtrot for pianola written by Casella in 1918:

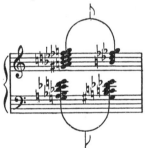

The composer—or, rather, the compiler—puts the thing more simply but less picturesquely in a note: 'Entres ces deux intervalles toutes les notes chromatiques frappées à la fois.'

Don't remind me that music is for the ear, not for the eye! Without forgetting

M 2

that, we may enjoy the comely page when we meet it. I sometimes think that the objection many musicians have to Tonic Sol-fa notation is subconsciously caused by its dull appearance. There is everything else to be said for it: it is practical, easy, and inexpensive to produce. But it is fatally new. It is a made system, like shorthand. Tonic Sol-fa has no past; whereas the staff was evolved. Look with a seeing eye at a page of the old notation and you get a good glimpse of the history of the art, and wherever there is history there is poetry. One is not merely fanciful in saying that however beautiful a piece of music is to the ear it is not without its appeal to the eye as well. The listener may think he has got out of a work all the enjoyment there is in it. But we who play and sing know better. We read from a set of symbols that is the growth of centuries; a true Esperanto, it is the only set of signs that is understood by educated folk in every civilized country. In the inexhaustible combinations and undulations of these signs is a beauty that is purely on paper. What other printed page so well bears looking at apart from its meaning?

SPIRIT OR LETTER?[1]

Symphonies 3, 5, 6, 7, 8, and 9 of Beethoven, adapted to the modern orchestra. Full and Miniature Scores (London: The Peabody Press).

WE may safely anticipate a warm welcome for this edition of some of the best works of a composer who, for want of such a revision, has for some years past met with neglect. Most of our readers will remember how, early in the twentieth century, an International Conference of conductors and other eminent musicians met at Brussels to consider the advisability of bringing certain passages in Beethoven's Symphonies into line with modern orchestral developments. At first the general feeling seemed to favour no more than a re-writing of some of the passages in which the composer had obviously been hampered by the imperfect instruments of his day. A minority wished to go further and add parts for trombone, tuba, contra-fagotto, and even the profundophone, the new machine-blown instrument which recently made such an impression at the Commonwealth Hall. This was opposed by the more conservative section of the Conference, but eventually the minority gained their point. Indeed, so completely did the pendulum swing across that the final decision was to re-score the works, leaving Beethoven's arrangement where possible— e.g. the string and drum parts, and most of the solo wood-wind passages. The task was entrusted to a committee of five well-known composers and conductors, whose names and reputations are sufficient guarantee that the difficult task has been performed with the due combination of reverence and skill. Not a note of the original has been altered, and the new edition contains no harmony that was not written, or obviously implied, by Beethoven. We should hesitate

[1] From the *Musical Times* of April 1, 2000.

to give an opinion on the merits of the new score if we had no more than the printed page to help us. But, as our readers know, the new versions have all been heard in London during the past few months, especially at the ten days' festival of old classical works directed by Dr. Cecilia Bompas, whose virile methods are remarkable, even in this age of masterly women conductors. The impression made was so profound as to disarm all but the most conservative criticism.

We have not space to consider the scores in detail, nor is such consideration necessary. It will suffice if we draw attention to a few of the passages which, as scored by Beethoven, have been an infliction to many ears during the past. Perhaps no movement gains more than the Finale to No. 7. We may venture to say that until the performance of the new version, nobody ever yet heard the theme:

at its first presentation, and at its reappearance on the return to the original key half-way through the movement. We were for a long while inclined to blame conductors for allowing the trumpets and horns to assert themselves too much, but of late we have come to the conclusion that the passage is really one of the cases in which Beethoven miscalculated the balance. Support to this view comes from Hector Berlioz,[1] who in his critical remarks on this Symphony says:

We should better appreciate the freshness of coquetry of this phrase . . . if the chords taken in upper parts

[1] A neglected and almost forgotten French composer (1803–69) who did much for the art of orchestration, even writing a treatise on the subject. We wish some of our conductors could see their way to reviving a few of his best works, such as the 'Queen Mab' Scherzo, his brilliant version of the 'Rakoczy' March, &c.

of the wind instruments were less dominating over the first violins singing in the medium register, whilst the second violins and violas accompany the melody below with a tremolo in double-stopping.'

For years we detested this portion of the movement, with the tonic and dominant blared out by the brass. We knew what the first violins were supposed to be playing, and we believed them to be playing it, for we saw them hard at work. But we have always had to take the result on trust until a few weeks ago, when we heard the theme given to all the violins, *ff*, in octaves. The hideous single notes of the old trumpets and horns have been superseded by chords for the complete brass, *mf*, with the syncopation of the original retained, of course. The high wood-wind parts remain, with the addition of an extra flute and clarinet, but now played *f* instead of *ff*. The lower string part consists of violas and 'celli divided. The gay song of the violins comes out with exhilarating effect against the rich background, and the movement at last lives up to its old title of 'the dance of humanity'. The only other part of this Finale that has been drastically revised is the section marked *fff*. This is almost, if not quite, the only time Beethoven employed such a direction, and we may fairly believe that (not to put too fine a point on it) he wanted a jolly good row. Perhaps contemporary ears thought it *was* a jolly good row. But to those of us accustomed to the sonority of a modern orchestra, the result was merely a *forte*. It may be said that a big effect depends more on the vigour of the thought expressed than on dynamics. We willingly concede the point; but, after all, the dynamic side is far more important than is sometimes imagined. Play the opening of the C minor Symphony *pp*, and observe the result. It is no longer Fate knocking at the door: it is merely a woodpecker enjoying himself. The fact is, pace and force are the making of many movements, just as long-drawn thought or delicacy is the prime consideration in others. Here we have a passage which obviously demands terrific pace and tremendous power. Beethoven got the first, and did his best to secure the second. But it was a bad best, with eight wood-wind and four (natural) brass instruments. The passage as now scored is a cataclysm over which Beethoven would have smacked his lips. The audience at its first performance were startled, several being removed suffering from shock. A few purists wrote to the papers protesting, but we believe that the result would have pleased the composer. He would probably have regretted the casualties—though we cannot be sure of that.

In this passage, as elsewhere, the greatest gain comes from the inclusion of the trombones and tuba. It has long been a matter for regret that Beethoven made so slight use of the former. Why, for example, in the fifth Symphony did he reserve them for the Finale? There are passages in the first movement that cry out for them. They are absent from the first movement of No. 9, and enter in the Scherzo to play a very humble part—only partly redeemed by the single high D with which the bass trombone so splendidly ushers in the D major section. Even in the Finale they are made to do far too much in the miserable role of support to the voice parts, for all the world like the serpent or ophicleide at the church blaring out the plainsong in order to help lame cantors over stiles. The fact is, the trombone (which we now recognize as the noblest voice in the orchestra) was under a cloud during most of Beethoven's life. It was mostly reserved for the wretched ecclesiastical duty mentioned above, and rarely had a chance to show its capabilities. Think of what modern composers do with a family of trombones in harmony *ppp*, and see what Beethoven missed by being born too soon!

We have mentioned the fifth Symphony, and are

reminded of certain shortcomings in the scoring that have hindered this work from achieving to-day the success which (if the records are to be trusted) it obtained during at least a century after the composer's death. Let the reader turn up the original version, and examine the following points. Look at the passage beginning at bar 114 of the slow movement. Here the bass strings have a florid version of the subject, while the rest of the strings, the wood-wind, and horns play repeated chords. Can anybody deny that the balance of the passage is upset by the vagaries of the trumpets? They have only two notes available during the eight bars, the C and G. The harmony of bars 1–2 is A flat, so they give us their tonic—C, the third of the orchestra's chord. Bar 3 and the first two beats of bar 4 modulate to B flat minor, so there is 'nothing doing' for the trumpets. The third beat of bar 4 gives us a dominant on G, and leads to a bar in C minor, whereupon the trumpets improve the occasion with G and C. But it is a mere flash in the pan, for in the next bar the music is again in B flat minor, which again puts the trumpets among the unemployed. Then comes the following (we reduce the harmony to its bare chords):

Here we have what may quite decently and truly be called a blasted tonic and dominant of C obtruded into the key of A flat, merely because the notes

happened to be lying round handy. Can anything
be more inept, especially in the final bar, where the
brilliant and dominating tone of the trumpet doubles
the leading-note? Prout [1] objected to this doubling,
and to the 'abrupt cessation of the trumpets in the
middle of a phrase', 'but' (he added) 'the fault, if fault
it be, rests not with Beethoven, but with the imperfection of the instruments for which he had to write'.
Exactly. Then why should not a matter of this kind
be rectified? There are many other examples—far
too many to refer to—which are a constant source of
irritation to the listener. These, we rejoice to feel,
have at last been put right.

The reader may ask how the thematic material of

[1] Ebenezer Prout, a famous theoretician, *b.* 1835; *d.* 1909.
The passages quoted are from his treatise *The Orchestra*,
vol. ii. Discussing the orchestration of Schubert's C major
symphony, he expresses what were no doubt the views of
musicians of his day—views that read curiously in these
less rigid times. In the peroration of the first movement
occurs, says Prout, 'a very grave miscalculation', the subject
being given to the wood-wind and horns, accompanied by
the strings, brass, and drums. As scored by Schubert, the
accompaniment hopelessly drowns the theme. Prout goes
on: 'Had Schubert ever had the opportunity of hearing
the Symphony played, he would probably have rescored the
whole of this peroration.' We may safely leave out the
'probably'. Prout then goes on to discuss various ways in
which the matter may be put right, only to dismiss them
with the observation that 'the retouching of the scores of
the great masters is objectionable on principle, and we must
take them, as men take their wives, "for better, for worse" '.
The analogy is shaky, for the wise husband loses no
opportunity of improving his wife, hopeless as the task too
often appears. But would the giving of the theme to the
trombones in unison, and so making the passage say what
Schubert obviously wanted it to say, be 'retouching'? Is it
not rather 'correcting' or 'remedying'? We should leave a
score untouched if there is any respectable weight of opinion
in favour of the original being correct or preferable in any
way. But in such cases as this, where there can be no two
opinions as to the composer's intentions, we must consider
the spirit rather than the letter.

the Symphonies bears the burden of the additional
orchestral parts. We know that certain types of music
lose more than they gain when subjected to such a test.
They become heavy rather than weighty. Without
exception, we think it will be found that the balance
here is all on the profit side. There are many passages
in which the thought was profound, but the expression
comparatively meagre. For example, this from the
first movement of No. 5:

We have always been impressed here, both by the
weighty chords and the antiphony. But we have also
felt that the means were too slender for the full realiza-
tion of Beethoven's intention. Apparently conductors
have felt the same, for they have generally adopted an
even more threatening attitude than usual in their
endeavour to extract from their players as much tone
as possible. The re-scored version gives a magnificent
effect, the antiphony now being between the whole of
the brass, and the strings and wood-wind. The effect
of the chords by eight horns, four trumpets, three
trombones, tuba, and profundophone is one of sombre
magnificence.

We hope we have said enough to indicate the
general lines on which the revisers have worked. We
believe that the best movements of these Symphonies
are as imperishable as anything in music. There can
be no more justification for continuing their performance on the inadequate lines of former days than
for playing Beethoven's keyboard works on a pianoforte of 1818. There is nothing specially sacred in the

actual scoring of Beethoven. He fixed certain broad principles, but it was inevitable that he could do no more, owing to many of the most important constituents of the orchestra being either uninvented or in an embryo stage. With an orchestral composer of to-day, the instrumentation is so important that it cannot be disturbed without injury. Indeed, too often the medium is more important than the matter—an unsound state of affairs. With Beethoven, the medium was often quite inadequate for the proper expression of the matter. The first of these discrepancies cannot be put right. Fortunately, the second can be. It has, we believe, been splendidly done in the edition under notice.

That such a step will escape censure is too much to expect. Already the storm is brewing. Last week the Society for the Protection of Antient Music met and passed a protesting resolution. We believe this and similar protests will be unavailing. When organists find Bach's works better on an old-fashioned tracker organ with heavy touch and few accessories; when pianists think the 'Appassionata' sounds better on a pianoforte of a hundred and fifty years ago than on a concert-grand of to-day; when a man who wants to go somewhere safely and quickly prefers a motor-car to an airplane; then, and not before, shall we believe that there are ears that can tolerate Beethoven played on the imperfect orchestra of his day—an orchestra for which he wrote, not because it was all his fancy painted it, but because it was that or nothing.

OUR EXCLUSIVES

First Exclusive: 'Do you never read the weeklies?'
Second Exclusive: 'Never. One feels that the only paper one could read with interest would be understood by so few people that it could never be published.'

Punch.

I HAVE just been reading an article by Miss Edith Sitwell on 'The Work of Gertrude Stein, a Modern Writer who brings Literature nearer to the apparently irrational World of Music'. Its interest lies chiefly in the fact that it shows certain of the extremist composers to be not alone in their amusing pretences to originality, and in their methods of work. Thus, one would have regarded it as obvious that a poet worthy the name always considered, not only the sense of his chosen words, but also their sound, singly and in combination. That is one of the prime differences between poetry and prose. To take two examples that at once come to mind: when Milton wrote:

And birds of calm sit brooding on the charmèd wave,

and Kipling:

And we drowsed the long tides idle till Thy trumpets
    tore the sea,

their choice of words was not guided by considerations of sense and metre only. They had their eye on euphony as well, and so gave us lines that we can enjoy as mere sound. But according to Miss Sitwell, this ingredient of poetry has just been discovered, or revived, by Gertrude Stein:

Miss Gertrude Stein is, I am convinced, one of the most important living pioneers, quite apart from the intrinsic value of her work. Language had come to be a threadbare thing, too tired to move—with words grouped together in their predestined families, blood-

173

less and timid. Miss Stein brings back life to these
dead creatures by what appears to us, when we read
her first, as an anarchic process. First she breaks down
the predestined groups of these words—their sleepy
family habits; then she rebrightens their use by building them into fresh shapes.

Mutatis mutandis, haven't we heard something like
this claimed on behalf of such composers as 'The
Six', and others?:—

Then, too, she is making new discoveries in what my
friend Mr. Robert Graves calls texture. In his book,
Contemporary Techniques of Poetry, published by the
Hogarth Press, Mr. Graves defines texture thus: 'The
term "texture" covers the relations of a poem's vowels
and consonants, other than rhymes, considered as mere
sound, and supplementing the rhythm and images. It
will . . . include the variation of internal vowel-sounds
to give an effect of richness; the use, perhaps, of liquid
consonants and labials and open vowels to give smooth-
ness, of aspirates and dentals to give force, of gutturals
to give strength; the careful use of sibilants, which are
to texture what salt is to food.' Miss Stein is making
inquiries in the exact result which is to be obtained
from this rough material.

Miss Stein need not search far in her inquiries.
Any collection of poetry, old or new, will provide
plenty of examples of all the points mentioned by
Mr. Graves.

Miss Sitwell admits that Miss Stein 'is, at present,
mainly a writer's writer—and often exceedingly difficult at that'. When, however, she goes on to claim that
'it is worth any amount of tiring work, to a writer,
to come to understand her', most of us will part
company with her. The main difficulty, we are told,
is that we are 'unaccustomed to abstract patterns being
built of words, though we have long been accustomed
to abstract patterns in the pictorial art and in music'.
Precisely; but music is not concerned with the expression of definite ideas, and with pictorial ones only

174

occasionally; whereas such expression is the prime function of words. Miss Sitwell goes on to explain that by abstract patterns in words she means

. . . the use of words, not for the sake of their philosophical content, but for the sake of discoveries whereby we may know more about the intrinsic atmosphere of each word, apart from its group-soul as part of a family.

Miss Stein, we are told,

. . . places words in contexts hitherto unknown, so as to gain their exact personality, deprived of that produced by their usual surroundings. This is not just playing about with words; it is an urgent necessity. There is always a connecting thread in each pattern, otherwise it would not be a pattern.

If the reader can see the 'urgent necessity' for the following 'pattern in words' he will enjoy it, though he is not likely to understand it:

> With the flag.
> With the flag of sets.
> Sets of colour.
> Do you like flags.
> Blue flags smell sweetly.
> Blue flags in a whirl.
> The wind blows.
> And the automobile goes.
> Can you guess boards.
> Wood.
> Can you guess hoops.
> Barrels.
> Can you guess girls.
> Servants.
> Can you guess messages?
> In deed.

Miss Sitwell admits that she does not find this as beautiful as other work: she quotes it because 'we see the processes of Miss Stein's thinking':

Flags make her think of irises. Flags make her think of the wind. The wind makes her think of the

175

speed of automobiles. Then she goes off on another track. Boards make her think of wood. Wood makes her think of barrels, of hoops, which make her see little girls, and so on. In much of her work she is too apt to take our sympathy and understanding for granted. She eliminates too much of her thought processes. As her work is exceedingly strange to those unaccustomed to it, if they are only made acquainted with the farthest end of this thinking and not with the gradual steps that led up to it, how can we hope that they will jump the intervening stages?

Again, doesn't all this sound familiar? Don't we know composers who make such a fetish of 'elimination of the unessential' that they end by becoming incoherent?

§

Here is another sentence that has an amusingly familiar ring:

It is unfortunately impossible to give a concrete explanation of Miss Stein's work. Either one understands it, or one doesn't. For it is a very crippling fact that there has not been sufficient preparation for this writer. She is often at the disadvantage of having gone so far ahead of our time that she is almost out of sight, and between her and her reader there is a gap.

This is real 'progress', and of a type that is painfully frequent in modern music.

Perhaps the most amusing thing in the article is Miss Sitwell's quoting of the following 'lovely phrases', and then solemnly trying to explain them:

Oh the bells that are the same are not stirring and the languid grace is not out of place and the older fur is disappearing. There is not such an end.

On this Miss Sitwell naïvely comments:

To my apprehension, this means (if we put it coarsely and roughly)—that youth has passed, spring comes again, with the same flower-bells upon the trees— but they no longer sound the same music—yet the older, furrier leaves have gone. I can imagine this phrase ending—though it does not end so, with the knowledge that soon we, too, shall be gone from the forests and the gardens. . . . That is what I read into this.

Here is another gem:

A pale rose is a smell that has no fountain, that has upside down the same distinction, elegance is not coloured, the pain is there.

Says Miss Sitwell:

This is, to me, an abstract pattern of very great beauty. The answer to the inquiry, 'What does this mean?' is—'It means exactly what a rose means.'

Still, in our reactionary way, we shall go on preferring a rose, by a long chalk.

However, this is a trifle to what Miss Stein can do in the way of mystification. In the following she leaves even Miss Sitwell in the dark:

Puzzle is more than a speck and a soiled collar. A pound is more than oatmeal and a new institution. A silence is more than occasional. It respects understanding and salt and even a rope. It respects a newsstand and it also it very also respects desert. All the ice can descend together.

There is a plaintive touch in Miss Sitwell's remark on this conglomeration:

I do not gain any idea whatsoever from this. My respect for Miss Stein makes me presume it is an abstract pattern with a thread, with a beauty, which I have not caught, but it appears to me quite incomprehensible, even as an abstract pattern.

It beats me also—in fact, very also.

§

Let me try my rude, unpractised hand at 'an abstract pattern':

It is true, it certainly is true and a coat, any coat, any dress, all dress, a hat, many hats, all colours, every kind of colouring, all this makes shadows longer and birds, makes birds, just makes birds. . . . Not much limping is in the back, not much limping is in the front, not much limping is circular, a bosom, a candle, an elegant footfall, all this makes daylight.

How's that for a beginner? . . .

Perhaps a Stein-ite objects that this is an absurd exaggeration, and that here, as in 'advanced' music, it is easier to poke fun than to imitate; that, in fact, the game is less easy than it appears to be. I hope such an objection is made, because it enables me to point out that this passage, so far from being an absurd exaggeration, is actually a quotation from Miss Stein! Miss Sitwell gives it, assuring us, truly, that 'it needs great experience to produce beauty in a passage like this'.

Yet one more analogy with some aspects of modern music is shown in the following remarks of Miss Sitwell:

Here, and in paragraphs like this, we find the danger of Miss Stein's method—a danger less to herself than to the people influenced by her. I hope the influence she is bound to have will be over able and experienced writers, not over the very young, incapable, and silly. These very young, incapable, and silly people who imitate and ruin all the modernist work of the time are a terrible problem. They mean well, but they hamper the movement, harass the real artists, and are, frankly, a great nuisance, as they bring ridicule on the modernist art.

Modernist art of this kind appears to be able to provide itself liberally with whatever it deserves in the way of ridicule. In fact, the more you look at it, the more certain you are that the pain is there, and that all the ice can descend together.

And, to make an end, here is a particularly choice example of Miss Stein's 'poetry':

Tingling they were they were they were tingling pink ice leads to trees they went twice they went

parrots fall gently across glass where they see Spain
they see nothing nothing is greener where are bronze
it cannot save from what is unbalanced in February
in March in April is undivided in three undivided it is
undivided it is indivisible it is.

Very well; who says it isn't?

CLICHÉ AND COMMONPLACE

PERIODICAL discussions on the *cliché* in music show a lack of agreement as to definitions. Some years ago Mr. G. H. Clutsam wrote an interesting series of articles in the *Musical Times*, giving numerous examples of what he described as *clichés*. But many of them were fine themes evolved from very simple and well-worn bases. To apply the derogatory term to such things would be to damn nearly all the world's great tunes. More recently Mr. Sydney Grew and Mr. Ernest Newman have gone over the ground, with results that were interesting, though there was a lack of agreement as to what constitutes a musical *cliché*. Mr. Grew wavered to such a degree as almost to contradict himself.

For example, speaking of cadences, he says:

Though a piece of music may end with a plain key-chord, yet that chord cannot be approached by the former harmonic steps—at least if *cliché* is to be avoided.

Later:

There is no need for excessive novelty in art. The once dead *cliché* may be made to flower again if the man puts his true self into his music.

So that, after all, there is life in the old cadence yet, always provided it is used by a composer who puts his true self into the job. This is so true that in saying it Mr. Grew goes a long way towards knocking the bottom out of a good deal of his argument. He says the same thing elsewhere. Thus:

It is obvious that 'pure music' must tend to become stereotyped in form; yet when an architectural feature is a necessity, and when the composition has life, the feature, though stereotyped, does not become a platitude.

In other words, a *cliché* ceases to be a *cliché* when handled by a composer of genius. But the verbal *cliché* can never be anything else, no matter who makes use of it, because, as Mr. Newman says: 'Ordinary language is a fixed thing, while the language of music is fluid.' The most threadbare progression may be transfigured by some slight rhythmical subtlety or an arresting harmonic touch, or by the manner in which it is approached or quitted. Hence the confusion that arises when we begin to argue from an analogy that at first sight appears convincing, but which ultimately breaks down.

Mr. Grew begins by talking about *clichés*, but soon gets switched on to quotations. He seems to justify this by the assertion that 'the *cliché* seems always to begin in quotation'. No doubt 'the devouring element', 'the sacred edifice', and a hundred other discredited tags began life with all the advantages of distinguished parentage and unexceptionable surroundings. They are now a pretentious cant-phraseology, as Mr. Grew says. But what he calls the 'real spell-words of genius' are on another footing, and are not so easily brought down in the world as he thinks. At what point may a Shakespearian quotation be said to have 'lost all allusive power, and passed into a pointless, meaningless, piece of abstraction'? Though used millions of times there are few or none that are not still alive when rightly employed—that is, as aids to a clear and vivid expression of thought. Only when dragged in (especially when prefaced by 'as the immortal Shakespeare says') do they lose caste. So much depends upon taste and judgement in the use of them that we may venture on a formula, and say that although every *cliché* is a quotation, a quotation (even the most familiar) is not necessarily a *cliché*. And here again we see there is no analogy between the commonplaces of literature and those of music. The former almost all begin as deliberate quotations,

whereas the latter are fashionable turns of melody, or
harmonic progressions, or the 'architectural features',
which, as Mr. Grew admits, are a necessity in pure
music.

§

Mr. Grew resisted the temptation to do more than
merely touch the subject of quotation in music. He
says the matter has never yet been adequately discussed by the critics. But the truth is that there is
hardly enough of such quotation to make lengthy
discussion worth while.

One of his few remarks on musical quotation
seems to show that he is still influenced by his
delusive literary analogy. He says 'quotation in music
easily descends into platitude'. However great the
danger may be in literary quotation it hardly exists
in music, because of the essential fluidity of the
medium. A musical phrase is rarely or never quoted
exactly. It is reharmonized, or its rhythm is modified,
or it is given a new aspect by being combined with
another theme. Moreover, it can rarely stand out
like a literary quotation because it has to be woven
into the texture of the music, and the process usually
involves some slight change in rhythm or harmony.
So far as there are any working principles in the
matter, modification is certainly one. This being so,
what we speak of as quotation is really allusiveness—
a more subtle thing.

If this be admitted, it rules out the danger of a
quotation's descent into platitude. A verbal phrase
is weakened by immediate repetition, and becomes
almost senseless with prolonged reiteration. But a
musical phrase not only survives repetition; it usually
gains thereby. Indeed, many themes of the briefer
type have little or no meaning until they have been
presented at least three or four times. The subject
of a ground bass may be an unimportant string of
notes when given out *in puris naturalibus* (a terrible

cliché this, perpetrated with malice prepense—hullo! there's another!) It may even be the veriest platitude. Yet it is anything but commonplace by the time a Bach or a Purcell has repeated it a score of times.

There are good reasons why composers have made so little use of quotation. Probably they realized that such allusions are as a rule far more liable to miss than to hit. A verbal quotation usually has the advantage of inverted commas or special type. Even without such aids it is rarely missed by the average reader, because the eye can take in at a glance not only the quotation but a good deal of the context as well; and if the quotation be not realized fully at first sight the reader can hark back and give himself another chance. The ear can hear only the sound of the moment; it knows nothing of what is ahead, and can call on the memory for little of what has gone before—a combined use of ear and memory possible only with the trained hearer. A musical quotation has to be very familiar, and must be given a good deal of prominence, before it has anything like the certainty of effect a verbal quotation can count upon. A further point so obvious as to need no more than mention is the fact that the classics of literature are more quotable than those of music, because they are more familiar to the average well-educated man. They have been a part of his education, whereas music . . .

§

Roughly speaking, notes and chords are the musical equivalents of letters and words. The fact reminds us of yet another disadvantage under which the musical quotation labours. What can be done with one chord —or even two? But a single word may call to the mind of the reader a wealth of associations. If you describe a certain man as a Pecksniff I not only have his whole character in a nutshell; I also taste again, in a lightning-flash of time, the pleasure derived from the parts of the book in which Pecksniff appeared. Probably the only chord that can of itself remind us of a particular work is the dissonance with which Beethoven ushers in the final section of the ninth Symphony. Most musicians would identify this readily, but the occasions on which it could be used with point are so few as to be negligible. Even so it would need to be led up to in some way. As one of the ingredients of a passage it might easily escape notice. It is doubtful if there is any pair of chords that can be quoted, but there are innumerable pairs of words that have only to be combined in order to make their effect with certainty. Used apart, 'multitudinous' and 'seas' are merely two words doing their duty as constituents of a sentence. But if I bring them together, everybody knows I am drawing on one of the mightiest lines in *Macbeth*. It is impossible to be so allusive in so small a space where music is concerned.

The most familiar of melodic fragments are apt to lose their identity unless accompanied by their original harmony. Even a wide departure from the original pitch may spoil them as allusions. For example, this passage reminds us of nothing in particular:

With a change of key to E flat:

it has a somewhat familiar sound, though not one musician in a hundred would identify it as a reference to one of the best-known of classics. Not until we present it thus:

can we count on its being easily recognized.

§

After all, the main reasons for literary quotation can never apply in music. We draw on an author for a phrase chiefly because we feel that it says once and for all in the best possible way something we in our turn wish to express, or because it backs up our own words, or because it gives the reader a short cut to our meaning. A composer who drew on another composer for (say) the treatment of a scale-passage because it struck him as being a good deal better than anything he himself could manage would find a harder term than 'quotation' applied to the process.

The verbal *cliché*, then, is unmistakable, and even the most skilful of craftsmen cannot make it appear better than it is. But we are so vague about the musical *cliché* that we may almost say there is no such thing. Thus Mr. Grew quotes a couple of cadences from Handel and Mozart, and says they are still beautiful and vital, but only when used by those composers. Let Pepusch and Abel write them, and they become 'withered' and 'like a bit of faded slang'.

Isn't this too sweeping? The cadences were the common property of the period. We still find pleasure in them when they are preceded by vital music. Sometimes this is the case with works by Handel and Mozart, but not always. Frequently the vital music is by the Pepusches and Abels, and the blighting and withering is done by the Handels and Mozarts, writing (as Mr. Grew says later) when they should have been resting.

We are again reminded of the haziness surrounding the subject when Mr. Grew says that 'the most vicious *cliché* in the middle of the nineteenth century was the chord of the diminished seventh, particularly as a modulatory step'. But a mere chord, like a word, cannot constitute a *cliché*. The excessive use of a striking chord or word is surely a mannerism. Nor is the whole-tone scale a *cliché*, as has been alleged. It is a basis, like any other scale, and differs from them only in being singularly limited in scope.

As the possibilities of fresh tonal combinations diminish, this question of commonplace is likely to be more frequently discussed, so it will be well to get our mind clear. I make my modest offering towards a solution by the suggestion that progressions usually described as *clichés* are the musical equivalents of such phrases as 'on the other hand', 'it goes without saying', 'as a matter of fact', 'beside the point', and scores of other useful tags. A writer or speaker with anything vital to say may use these liberally and give no impression of platitude. Similarly, a composer may be original and yet employ the modulatory links, approaches to cadences, and melodies or figures based on scale and arpeggio passages. The most ordinary series of common chords may be made into a thing of beauty. The well-known 'Ave Maria' commonly attributed to Arcadelt is compounded almost entirely of such chords in root positions—that is, used in a way that the elementary harmony student regards as necessarily productive of dull squareness.

Anxiety to avoid these simple and natural constituents leads almost invariably to stilted and affected phraseology, both in literature and music. It is like trying to pay one's bus fares with nothing but pound

notes. At such times the humble copper coin is a
boon. When writing or composing we should not
despise the occasional use of small change in getting
from point to point. Of course if there are no points,
we need not make the journey.

II

How far these legitimate commonplaces may be
made to suffer a sea-change by means of instrumental
and other resources is a further consideration suggested by Mr. Newman's two quotations from Balfour
Gardiner and Puccini. Mr. Newman agreed with
Mr. Grew's description of this passage (from an early
work by Balfour Gardiner):

as 'a specimen of the harmonic *cliché* of the first
decade of the present century'. I should have described the addition of a foreign note to a string of
common chords as a mannerism rather than a *cliché*.
The genuine harmonic *cliché* is some such progression
as that with which 'The Rosary' begins its bilious
progress—in itself a beautiful bit of colour when used
in a less obvious manner. This by the way. As Mr.
Newman says, the sequence of added notes strikes us
now as entirely lacking in originality. He then quotes
this from Puccini:

and says, 'It never strikes us as being a *cliché*.' I have not heard 'Suor Angelica', but I went through the pianoforte score of the work soon after its publication, and I remember this very passage striking me as a double-barrelled commonplace—a stereotyped fragment of bell-music supported by triads, each one bearing a pimple in the shape of an added note. On paper, and played on the pianoforte (especially if put into the same key), there is but a pinpoint difference in the value of the examples on p. 187. In both cases the procedure is the same. The pinpoint goes to the second, perhaps, because it is more pleasing melodically; but, as we see, its little bit of tune is borrowed from the belfry.

Some of Mr. Newman's readers must have been puzzled at his saying of the Balfour Gardiner phrase that 'to-day, as a rule, nothing sounds more obvious, more ludicrously unoriginal than this sort of sequence', and of the second, 'it never strikes us as being a *cliché*'. The explanation, of course, is to be found in the orchestration. Puccini begins by announcing the chime twice, first on the bells, second on the celeste. The second passage quoted on p. 187 is then given to the strings, the tune and chords played by first and second violins *divisi*, with a solo 'cello playing the lower F, D, E, C, &c., *pizzicato*, the added notes being given to the violas. Later the passage is scored for strings in eight parts, with softly clashing seconds in octaves picked out on the harps:

This is an excellent example of a phrase trite when played on a keyboard instrument, with only one colour and sonority for all the parts, but fascinating when shared by even so few instruments as in this case.

188

§

Although, as we see, the salvation of the Puccini passage lies in the scoring, it gains also from its significance as a dramatic element. Mr. Newman says it suggests, 'in a curious, inexplicable way, the blending of peace and pain in the atmosphere of the convent'. It does, but there is nothing inexplicable about it, and I'll be bound that if you had buttonholed Mr. Newman at Covent Garden while the passage was being played and had asked him why it suggested this blending, he would have given you the reason readily enough. The bell-like theme suggests the convent, the common chords security and peace, and the added note hints at the pain from which even the cloistered cannot entirely escape. Nothing subtle about this, you will say. Exactly; but Puccini was the most successful stage composer of his day precisely because he was not subtle.

We see, then, that the platitude of the pianoforte not only blossoms on being transferred to the orchestra; shifted from the drawing-room to the operatic stage it becomes charged with a power of suggestion as convincing as anything in pictorial art. So brilliant and dashing an adventure can very rarely happen to a verbal platitude. Occasionally a Shaw or a Chesterton will take some well-worn expression and use it in a freakish manner, a commonplace changing into a cracker. But such feats are not only rare: they are almost invariably confined to the humorous, whereas their musical counterparts have unlimited emotional possibilities.

The late Herbert Campbell—or was it Dan Leno?—made a great success with a song the burden of which was 'It's the seasoning that does it'. To a great extent, it always *was* the seasoning, in music as in everything else. The only change has been in the kind of seasoning. We are apt to generalize and say that the old composers always wrote tunes, and that

the modern ones, finding the melodic possibilities of
the scale exhausted, are driven to serving up thematic
crumbs so flavoured with harmonic and instrumental
sauce as to pass for highly original dishes. But the
best works of the old writers are by no means those
that appear to be richest in thematic invention. What
to-day are the most vital portions of Beethoven's
fifth Symphony? Many of us have little use for the
second subject of the first movement, or for any part
of the Andante, and we can even spare the Finale.
All these are definitely tuneful. The most arresting
moments in the work are those concerned with the
hammering motive of the first movement, the bustling
bit of fugato in the Scherzo, and the passage over the
drum leading into the Finale. The first is as insignificant a scrap as can easily be found, the second scores
heavily by an effect not really musical—the rough and
tumble of the double-basses playing so quickly that
we can scarcely hear the notes for the noise—and the
third hints rather than speaks, and grips us with the
vague menace of something round the corner. These
two latter are typical Beethoven seasoning—a frank,
uncouth humour, and a significant use of the drum.
The four-note motive from which the greater part of
the first movement is evolved still holds us because of
the dramatic effect produced by its insistence—also
a kind of seasoning. True, it owes a great deal to the
'Fate knocking at the door' story. Yet Beethoven is
said to have noted it down from the cry of some small
wild-fowl—a yellow-hammer, wasn't it? But how
many hearers think of the yellow-hammer? They are
all poets for a brief spell, and invest the music with a
significance probably more profound than the composer ever gave it. What verbal commonplace can
ever come to mean so much as this trivial bird-call?
It is as if such an expression as 'I'll trouble you for
the salt' suddenly became charged with tremendous
and shattering import. You would forget the salt, and

would instead speculate as to the strange power that
has in a moment changed a phrase into a spell. If
a composer happens to be at hand, he will tell you that
he and his fellows have done the thing so often that
it is taken for granted.

One of the infallible signs of greatness in a composer
is this power of making something from nothing.
Some of the finest of Bach's fugues have short subjects of no moment until the old man gets to work
on them. He and Purcell could take a scrap of the
chromatic scale, put it in the bass, and produce a
'Crucifixus' and Dido's 'When I am laid in earth'.
Handel saw that the plagal cadence was the very thing
for a shout of Hallelujah, and shouted accordingly,
and we still shout with him, though the thematic
material of the whole chorus is elementary, and the
music hardly ever leaves the tonic and dominant.
Beethoven heard a yellow-hammer deliver a major
third, and in his turn produced his best-known
symphonic movement. Make a list of twenty of the
best known of the countless examples of this strange
power of transmutation: you will then realize the
prime difference between the verbal and the musical
cliché—genius can do nothing with the first; it works
miracles with the second.

III

'Something from nothing' . . . One would have
thought that there could be no question as to a great
composer's ability to evolve a fine movement from an
insignificant theme. Yet the point was warmly debated recently by Mr. Scholes and the present writer,
with interventions from the onlookers. It was clear
that musicians differed as to the commonplace no less
than as to the *cliché*. Much depends on whether we
look at a theme before or after a composer has worked
his miracle with it. For example, Mr. Scholes and
the rest of us agree that this :

is a tremendously significant motive. But *was* it before
Beethoven wrote the fifth Symphony? If there be
such a thing as a cuckoo afflicted with a stammer,
this is, in fact, the kind of call he would utter.
Beethoven, we know, used to extemporize on it, just
as d'Aquin and many other composers have amused
themselves with the normal cuckoo-call. But the
notes *m m m d* were of little moment, even in Beethoven's hands, till the C minor Symphony came into
being, and their present significance is quite fortuitous.

Mr. Scholes suggested that had the theme been
changed to:

it would have been so weakened that even Beethoven
could have made nothing great out of it. Arguing
from an hypothesis is perhaps fruitless, but I may
point out that as a good deal of Beethoven's most
striking use of the theme is derived, not from the
intervals, but from the rhythm, the alteration would
matter very little. Indeed, so far from weakening its
germinal possibilities, it would have increased them.
Had the yellow-hammer sung:

Beethoven would probably have done a great deal
with some such derivative as:

which appears to contain more possibilities than

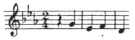

However, the main point is that Beethoven has evolved a great movement from a theme that in itself was of no importance, though, thanks to the composer, it is now one of the most suggestive in music.

§

Bach inevitably comes into a discussion of this kind. Mr. Scholes mentioned some fugue subjects, both strong and weak, and expressed his conviction that good fugues are never produced from poor subjects. One almost agrees with him here, because a fugue depends, far more than does a free movement, upon the quality of its subject. A sonata movement is so largely a matter of development that a long work may be concerned far more with the derivatives of the subjects than with the subjects themselves, whereas the essence of the fugal form lies in its insistence on the subject, presented (usually without change) in a constantly varying polyphonic texture. Let us use Mr. Scholes's simile of the sermon and text: in a free movement the matter may be discursive. One thing brings up another, and the preacher may follow and develop the most promising of them, though the relation to the text may escape any but the closest observer. In a fugue the text may be left for a brief space (the episode), but the discourse must constantly return to it, showing it in a new aspect, either through its relations to other constituents (counter-subjects) or by regarding it from a fresh point of view (inversion, augmentation, diminution). Even the episodes are as a rule not entirely free, for in a well-behaved fugue they are derived from the subject or counter-subject. A fugue, then, cannot fairly be brought into the

argument, though there would be no difficulty in
showing that even here Bach has more than once or
twice done wonders with trifling material.

The organ Toccata in F, being largely fugal and
canonic, is an outstanding example, the whole of this
gigantic movement of four hundred and thirty-eight
bars being derived from these two insignificant
motives:

(We may even regard *b* as an augmentation of the
first half of *a*.)

Although Mr. Scholes refused to admit that the
Toccata is a success (he holds it to be 'one of Bach's
poorer pieces'—an opinion that will find few backers),
I still regard it as one of the most conclusive examples
of 'something from nothing'.

From both *a* and *b* come some derivatives that most
of us regard as magnificent. But not Mr. Scholes. He
even denies the possibility—or, at least, the probability—of such an evolution. He says: 'A stream does
not rise higher than its fount, and the derivatives of
a theme are not likely to be better than the theme
itself.' The analogy fails every time we draw water
from a tap, for we see that, given due pressure, water
does so rise. And in music the genius of the composer
supplies the pressure that changes a mere dribble into
a fountain. If Mr. Scholes wants to see a derivative
improving on its origin, he need only look again at the
Beethoven movement:

And, again, in the Scherzo:

Aren't these derivatives better than the stuttering cuckoo-call?

The fact is, the composer, above all creative artists, has this power of evolving something from nothing, and as a general rule the greatest composers are those who have this power in the greatest degree. Had Browning been a better musician, he would have perhaps had in mind this, rather than the making of the triad, when he wrote the last verse of 'Abt Vogler'. 'A commonplace?' he would have made the composer say:

Give it to me to use! I mix it with brain and with heart;
And there! Ye have heard and seen: consider and bow
    the head!

WHY NOT PLAIN ENGLISH?

... Let us have ... English—plain, perspicuous English—
... Ours is a noble language, a beautiful language. ... He who
uses a Latin or a French phrase where a pure old English word
does as well, ought to be hung, drawn, and quartered for high
treason aginst his mother-tongue.
   ROBERT SOUTHEY (Letter to William Taylor).

ALTHOUGH Southey, when writing the above, had in mind the purely literary aspect of this question, his words may without much strain be applied to a good deal of our musical terminology.

Among our natural tendencies of to-day is one towards the formation of unofficial societies for the Propagation of British Products. The ground covered is a wide one, ranging from hardware to music. In many cases nice questions of tariffs, trades unionism, &c., will be involved, and we may find that the question of 'looking after number one' is by no means so simple a matter in a national as in an individual sense. There is, however, one small question that crops up from time to time which we musicians might quite well settle for ourselves with nothing but good results. Hasn't the time come for the general use of our own language for directions as to performance and for titles? The change would not be an expression of narrowness or insularity, still less of antipathy to any other race. It is merely a matter of common sense and of natural pride in our own tongue. We may well be diffident about some things, but when language and literature are mentioned, we have cause to hold our head up and fear comparison with none of our neighbours.

Is there any practical reason why we should go on peppering our pages with scraps of Italian? Twenty years ago there was something to be said in favour of such a proceeding. Italian terms were in general

European use for the purpose, and had become recognized as a kind of musical Esperanto. But this use has gradually diminished. A glance at modern French and German music shows that composers are more and more making use of their own tongue. Even English composers have been following suit, but in most cases they appear to find the shedding of their Italian shackles difficult, and after a few English words we generally find a *rallentando* or *sostenuto* creeping in.

As a specimen of this hybrid method, I take up the first piece of modern English music that lies to hand, a set of three pieces by one of our most representative composers.

On page 3 we find the direction, *un poco più di moto*, and on page 8 *a shade quicker*. On page 9 we have in three bars *tempo primo, very slow*, and *poco ad lib*. Here is another work, with such a medley as *retard, slightly detached, non legato*, and, best of all, *very legato*! Can you see a German writing *sehr loud*, or a Frenchman, *très quick*? Presumably the composer wrote *very*, and then could find no English for *legato*. But if German and French composers can (and do) say *sehr gebunden* and *très lié*, surely we English might summon up courage enough for *well tied* or *bound*.

A glance at other recent English music shows similar inconsistency. Is this due to any deficiency in our language? I have just spent a half-hour with a dictionary of musical terms, and so far have sought in vain for an Italian term in common use that has no satisfactory English equivalent. (I recently read with surprise in a musical journal discussing this subject that there was no English word to use instead of *ritardando*!)

§

Let us consider one of the most frequently used of directions. A composer who wishes for a decrease in the speed of a movement writes *rallentando, ritardando, tardando, lentando, stentando, strascicando, ritasciando*, *meno mosso*, or *ritenuto*. But we have an English form of the second in the list—'retard' (says Nuttall), 'to diminish the velocity of'. What more do we need? And it is worth noting that an English teacher, in giving a counterpoint lesson, will speak of 'retardation', but when teaching the pianoforte, will relapse into Italian and demand a *ritardando*!

Is there any reason why we should go on using *accelerando*, and half a dozen similar terms, when our own 'accelerate' will answer the purpose equally well? The musical dictionary gives us fourteen Italian terms for 'dying away', nine for 'gracefully', eleven for 'mournfully', over twenty for various degrees of 'fast' (all of which can be indicated by such words as 'very', 'rather', 'less', &c.), ten for 'passionate'—but there is no need to lengthen the list.

There may be doubt as to the best English equivalent in some cases. As a substitute for *crescendo* 'increase' is perhaps better than Percy Grainger's 'louden'; his 'slacken' is possibly better than 'retard', but 'slacken much' is certainly to be preferred to 'slacken lots'. For *diminuendo* we want nothing better than 'diminish' or 'decrease'.

We might well, too, revive the use of such racy old directions as 'cheerful' and 'lively'. Another delightful word so far too little used is 'merrily'—there is a laughing ripple in the very sound. But English composers will have none of it. They bid us play or sing *giocoso*, *giocosamente*, *gaiamente*, &c., but 'gaily' or 'merrily' hardly ever. So we haven't after all changed much since John Cooper about 1600 found it worth while to be known as Coperario.

There are musicians among us who laugh at Cooper, but who still signify their wish that a pause should be short by writing over it *piccolo* or *pochettino*. A French composer would write *court*, and why we English cannot be content with 'short' is one of the things past finding out.

198

It may be asked, what about abbreviations? The commonly used Italian ones are here placed side by side with their English allies:

rit(*ard*)   = ret(ard)
accel(*erando*) = accel(erate)
dim(*inuendo*) = dim(inish)
cres(*cendo*)   = inc(rease)
p(*oco*) *a p*(*oco*)= l(ittle) by l(ittle)
sost(*enuto*)   = sust(ained)

When we come to the universally employed letters for directions as to loud and soft, we may pause before suggesting the use of *ml* for *mf*, or *ms* for *mp*. Those in the field may be allowed to stand, as being a convenient kind of shorthand. This is inconsistent, but we need not worry over one more small anomaly being added to the already liberal supply with which our notation is decorated.

On the whole, the more the matter is considered, the more there is to be said in favour of using plain English for directions. The use of Italian terms is a mere convention; there was never much to be said for it, and its perpetuation to-day is a ridiculous affectation.

§

The question of titles is not so easy. There are two heads to this part of the subject: (*a*) the use of English titles by English composers, and (*b*) the translation of foreign titles. The first of these should admit of no question. It is amazing that the bad old tradition should have lasted so long.

Préludes Romantiques
pour
le
piano
par——

par whom do you think? Not Jean le Brun, but just plain John Brown. If John had any good

grounds for supposing that his romantic preludings
would reach the ears of the French public there might
have been some excuse for his dropping into French
—though not much. But his work was rarely heard
outside the island on which he conferred distinction.
This kind of title-page was common in our young days
and you may say that we have changed for the better.
We are changing, but slowly. The only recently
published English music within my reach happens to
be for the organ. I turn over a pile and find the
following, mostly by composers who are unlikely to
have any public abroad—or outside their own parish
in some cases: 'Rêverie' (there are about six of these
tone-poets who apparently think 'Rêverie' is better
than 'Reverie'!), 'Mélancolique', 'Chant du Matin',
'Phantasie', 'Chanson Pastorale', 'Fantasie [*sic*] Pré-
lude', 'Sincérité', 'Prière', 'Grande Marche Solennelle'—it would be easy to treble the list, but I refrain.
I add, however, four particularly choice specimens—
'Brise d'Eté' (what in the world is the matter with
'Summer breeze'?), 'Wohin?' 'Geistliche Träume',
and 'Friedenshoffnung'. Let me repeat that all the
above titles are used on music written by Englishmen
and published recently in this country. Where should
they gather flowers of speech for titular uses if not
from the tongue in which they were born? Echo
answers 'Wohin?'

At a recent concert some new sketches for pianoforte
were played. They were composed by an Englishman,
played by an Englishman to an English audience, and
were, as a natural consequence, called 'Esquisses'.

The absurdity of this sort of thing is so obvious
that there is no need to dwell on it further. When we
come to the question of translations of foreign titles,
there are difficulties, it is true, but they are not
numerous. In most cases it is easy to find an English
equivalent, and common sense would seem to suggest
the use of it. For instance, as an extreme example

of ridiculous sticking to the original, take the case of an organ recital given a few months back at a village church. The organist played Schumann's Four Sketches for pedal pianoforte; what the rude fore-fathers of the hamlet thought when their programme told them that they were listening to 'Vier Skizzen' I should very much like to know. Here are a few items culled from recent concert and recital pro-grammes: 'Vorspiel', 'Carneval', 'Minuet Nuptiale', 'Im Garten', 'Mélodie', 'Marche Funèbre', 'Overture Solennelle', 'Chant sans paroles', 'Rhapsodie Hon-groise', 'Chanson d'Eté', 'Mélodie Lyrique', 'Vor-spiel, Die Meistersinger', 'Trauer Marsch'—here again the material is too much for the space. Some-times the titles are a bi-lingual affair. In the pro-grammes of recent orchestral concerts in London we find 'The Pathétique', 'Rhapsody Hongroise', 'Sym-phonic Fantasie', and 'Concerto grosse'. If we *must* use foreign tongues, we might at least avoid such mixtures as these. But surely when the works are played in England they might be called by English names. Those responsible for the programmes of our chief orchestral concerts are on the whole adopting this policy, but there is a lack of consistency, so that it is still possible to find on the same page 'The Flying Dutchman' and 'Die Meistersinger'; 'Academic Festival' and 'Die Zauberflöte'; 'Entrance of the Gods into Walhalla' and 'Huldigung's Marsch', and many others.

All the foreign titles so far mentioned present no difficulty to the translator. A glance through a long list of standard works shows a mere handful that are better left alone. The *Musical Times* for August 1915 contained an extract from a weekly newspaper in which this point was raised, with a list of titles in their foreign and English forms. The majority of these were unexceptionable, but one or two examples were less happy, and served to show that the question is

not always easily settled. 'L'après-midi d'un Faune'
appears as 'A Faun's afternoon'—a bald statement
containing none of the suggestiveness of the original.
'The afternoon of a Faun' is worse, combining matter-
of-factness with a hint of the pen of the gardener's
niece. In such cases we want something more than
a translation. Here the solution is perhaps some
such compound title as 'Afternoon in the woods: the
Faun'. It has the double merit of reading well and of
presenting something helpful to the mind's eye.

There are a few titles that somehow refuse to sound
quite right in English. Why is 'Moment musical' an
excellent title for a short piece, and 'A musical
moment' merely ridiculous? Why do 'Valse Triste'
and 'Chanson Triste' appear uncomfortable in translation? And in cases where Italian verbs and adjec-
tives have become substantivized, e.g. Adagio, Presto,
Andante, &c., and used as titles, one hardly likes to
suggest a change. On paper the effect would not be
bad, but to speak of playing a 'Slow', or a 'Rather
Fast', would be to incur a charge of eccentricity.

We need not be eccentric or fussy over the matter.
All we have to do is to use our own language, unless
we are satisfied that a foreign one will express our
meaning *better*. We shall probably be surprised at
the rarity with which English fails to meet the case.
Certainly there will be no need for the repetition of
such an absurdity as that quoted in the *Musical Times*
extract mentioned above: a war-time meeting at
which a peer, a member of Parliament, a major-general,
and some well-known public speakers harangued their
fellow-Britons on their duty, concluding with the
performance by a crack band of the British Army of
a work announced in the programme as 'Zweite
Hungarischer Rhapsodie'! It would have been a
fitting sequel to such a fatuous proceeding if the
assembled patriots had got on to their hind legs and
signified their enjoyment by shouts of 'Hoch! Hoch!'

ACTIONS AND REACTIONS

'SONATA, what do you want of me?' asked Fontenelle, and, like jesting Pilate, seems not to have waited for an answer. Similarly, Tolstoy over and over again had searchings of heart: 'Music is a dreadful thing. What is it? What does it do to me?' Probably an exact answer can never be made, because most of the factors lie outside the scope of science. But an interesting effort has been made (1927) in America, and the results are worth the attention of all interested in psychology and musical reaction.[1]

The book, says the Introduction, 'is at once a response and a challenge':

It is a response to the inquiry which any thoughtful listener makes, 'What is this music doing to me?' At the same time it is a challenge to science to explain more accurately than has yet been done the nature and the mysteries of musical effects.

Perhaps I am not a thoughtful listener. Anyway, questions of this kind have never bothered me. The longer I live, and the more music I hear, the less is my concern as to its meaning and effects, and (I add this less I be accounted *blasé*) the greater my enjoyment and the wider my sources of pleasure in the art. This is probably the experience of most musicians, and it is mentioned here at the outset as a point that is too little regarded by psychologists and other explorers into regions that are perhaps after all best left uncharted. Nevertheless, none of us can afford to ignore such charts as are available, though, in the nature of things, the musician can never agree entirely with the scientist's conclusions, because only the

[1] *The Effects of Music.* A series of Essays, edited by Max Schoen (Kegan Paul).

musician realizes fully that the qualities which matter
most in music are those that are least explainable—
if, indeed, they can ever be explained at all.

§

The experiments recorded in this volume were as
comprehensive as possible, and consisted of the performance, *per* gramophone, of various sets of works,
the hearers being provided with an elaborate *questionnaire* on which to record their impressions. Investiga-
tions were also made concerning the effect of certain
types of music on the blood-pressure and heart. The
gramophone was the chosen medium because it ensured
a standardized performance: no player, singer, or
conductor worth his salt can guarantee this. But can
any listener guarantee a standardized hearing? Is there
not, in fact, a greater margin of variability in the
hearer, if only for the reason that his powers of con-
centration are likely to be less developed than those
of the highly-skilled performer? This seems to have
been recognized by the experimenters, who guarded
their subject from distraction as far as possible. He
was seated in a comfortable arm-chair with his back
to the gramophone. Not for him the cramped knees,
the hard seat, and pinched equators that the more
globular among us endure in the concert-hall! He was
even 'tuned-up', so to speak:

Before a person first listened at any sitting, he was
always initially given a record to hear (not one of those
he was to hear later) in order to become accustomed to
the experimental conditions.

In some cases he was alone, too, with no coughs but
his own, and no rustlings of programmes or distrac-
tions of any kind.

If we all listened to music under these happy conditions, the tabulated results would be more valuable
than they are. In time, no doubt, wireless will enable

us all to reproduce such ideal circumstances, from the comfortable arm-chair downwards. Yet—so delicately hinged are our mental adjustments!—even then we shall be unable to say exactly what music does for us, because the very fact of being provided with an elaborate form whereon to record our impressions must induce a touch of self-consciousness. To many, the effort to express themselves on paper will be a worry; others, with facility in that way, will affect to see more in the music than they really do. A perfectly receptive mind for experimental purposes seems therefore to be impossible; the mirror can hardly be unclouded, and so its reflections can never be exact.

A point concerning the use of the gramophone deserves a word: it made possible a standardized performance, and it had further advantages in regard to immediate repetition of an entire work or of certain salient passages. But surface noises, and its lapses from purity of tone and from exact reproduction of tone-colours, were a serious disability. Hence some curious findings. Thus, in one set of experiments, the victims were asked to express, by means of figures, the proportions of enjoyment derived from Rhythm, Melody, Design, Harmony, and Tone-Colour. The composers included Handel, Bach, Beethoven, Wagner, Liszt, Brahms, and Debussy. Can the reader guess which scored most heavily under 'Tone-Colour'? Of course he can: I hear him reply, in crowds, 'Wagner!' Wrong: try again! 'Liszt?' Wrong: make a third and last shot! 'Debussy.' No: the poll is headed by Handel! Wagner scored heavily in Rhythm (347), Melody (674—yet a few years ago he 'couldn't write a chune'!), Design (295), and Harmony (400). In Tone-Colour he could manage only a mere 217. Clearly the gramophone, marvellous as it is, is less good than we thought it to be in the reproduction of instrumental timbres. This is proved by the fact that all the Tone-Colour figures were comparatively low. (Of course the trained musician makes good its defects mentally, which the subjects in the experiment were probably less able to do.)

The Handel total for Tone-Colour (235) raises an interesting point. The eight pieces by which he was represented were all taken from 'The Messiah'. (Here, by the way, is exposed a weakness in the experiment. What basis of comparison is there between a selection from an eighteenth-century oratorio and a series of extracts from Wagner?) One would have expected Handel to receive large figures for everything but tone-colour and (possibly) harmony. Yet all are low compared with those given to other composers. The whole table is worth quoting:

Composer	Rhythm	Melody	Design	Harmony	Tone-Colour
Handel	119	144	137	65	235
Bach	446	736	727	352	179
Haydn	211	217	181	61	73
Mozart	135	203	153	59	76
Beethoven	492	522	338	332	190
Schumann	827	839	227	356	74
Chopin	382	466	220	234	114
Mendelssohn	134	202	78	116	49
Wagner	347	674	295	400	217
Liszt	133	173	59	157	92
Brahms	212	192	124	146	37
MacDowell	135	162	34	152	34
Debussy	94	100	22	124	42

'It is not improbable that vocal tone-colour attracts more than instrumental tone-colour,' says the book, in attempting to explain the curious fact of Handel reaching his highest total in the column where we should look to find his smallest. It is more than probable: it is certain—at all events so far as the less sophisticated hearer is concerned.

Such a hearer responds to vocal music from the start —partly, of course, because of the words and their associations. Instrumental tone-colour rarely interests him save in its more glaring primary aspects. That is why chamber music, with its countless subtleties and shadings, usually strikes him as being 'dry'. This by the way. My point here is that the experimenters seem to have given too little thought to the big part played by familiarity and association of ideas. A separate column should have been allotted to this factor. All the hearers, we may be sure, knew every note of 'The Messiah' extracts, and enjoyed them mainly for that reason. Hence Handel's low totals in the first four columns; for apparently a good many of the listeners, being unable to account for their pleasure under the headings Rhythm, Melody, Design, and Harmony, fell back on Tone-Colour as the way out. A column headed 'Association of Ideas', or 'Familiarity', would have given the desired outlet. Even so, Handel comes badly off in the matter of grand total—a fact which seems to indicate that the appeal of vocal music is after all less potent than it is thought to be. And look at Schumann's enormous figures! Twenty-five of his works were played, including the whole of the 'Carnaval', each number of which was counted separately. Presumably the remainder were also pianoforte music, but no information is given. In fact, save for 'The Messiah' and 'Carnaval', the titles of the music used in this particular experiment are not stated—an omission which deprives the figures of a good deal of significance.

§

In the tests on 'The Mood Effects of Music' a smaller selection was used, and titles are forthcoming. It was a mixed bag—'Stars and Stripes for ever', 'To a wild rose', 'Blue Danube Waltz', 'He shall feed His flock', 'Love's old sweet song', and the Bach-Gounod 'Ave Maria', &c.

A more interesting experiment was that concerning 'The effect of immediate repetition on the pleasant-

ness and unpleasantness of music'. A section of a
record was played:

After an interval of thirty seconds, allowing time for
re-setting, it was repeated. The procedure was con-
tinued until five performances of the section had been
given. Then, after an interval of two minutes, another
section, of a different record, was similarly treated.
Eight records were used in an experiment. The sections
were always the first part of the records, and so chosen
as to occupy about one minute in playing. They were
always long enough to allow for the completion of a
theme, and thus possessed musical completeness.

The audiences consisted of groups of various sizes
up to twenty-four, and their job was to note and
describe the changes in their attitude to the music as
the repetitions went on. The works were in four
grades: 'Severely classical; serious popular classical;
easy popular classical; and popular.' There was a
further division into fast and slow.

The difficulty of classifying music in this way is
shown by the fact that the four 'severely classical' works
consisted of (fast) the first movement of the 'Un-
finished' and the Fugue from Beethoven's C major
String Quartet; and (slow) a Mozart Andante and
Wagner's 'Träume'. None of these can be called
'severe', for even the Fugue has the attractions of
energy, pace, and great rhythmic vitality. In fact,
practically all the pieces mentioned in the three cate-
gories of classical are interchangeable. Only when
we come to the section headed 'Popular' are we safe
with two fox-trots and two waltzes. In the face of
this, it is clear that we must not hastily decide as to
the comparative attractiveness of the 'severely' classical, and the 'serious' and 'easy' popular classical. The
'severe' has a way of becoming merely 'serious' after
a few hearings, and 'easy' after a good many more.

I have not space to go into the results of this experiment, especially as they are given almost entirely

in forbidding columns of figures, not without fractions. Boiled down, they merely tell us elaborately what we already know: that so-called popular music makes an immediate effect which is weakened by repetition, whereas classical music does the reverse. Similarly, with a wealth of learned terminology, it is demonstrated that a lullaby has a markedly soothing effect on a patient suffering from palpitation, and that the 'Pathetic' Symphony and similar febrile music is 'not recommended for individuals who are fatigued, depressed, or ill'. (This is followed by a delicious recommendation, apparently delivered in all seriousness: 'It might be employed to subdue hilarity in individuals or masses of people.') Most of the discoveries in this book are the sort of thing that you and I have always known instinctively. But feeling things in your bones is (like what the soldier said) not evidence. These experiments, despite obvious flaws (some of them inevitable), provide both evidence and valuable data.

Before closing the volume, I extract one or two details that will probably be of interest. Here is an addition to our stock of programme-music absurdities. We all know what a mere title will do in helping out a piece of descriptive music. We know, too, what happens sometimes when the labels get mixed:

The effect of the title in suggesting associations was amusingly shown in one case where the listener had made a mistake in identifying the selection. The reverse side of the record 'In a Clock Shop' is devoted to a 'Hunting Scene'. The person had confused the two selections, and reported rich imagery illustrative of hunting instead of the imagery so appropriately evoked by the Clock Shop record!

This would be incredible had it not been stated in a scientific volume.

§

The history of music may be said to be one long process of getting used to things. Familiarity is the solvent: the discord of yesterday is the concord of to-day. This fact is also demonstrated by experiment:

Chords, which at first are decidedly unpleasant, grow less unpleasant as they are heard again and again. (This change must not be confused with the change that they undergo when responded to as a part of their environment.) Several hundred repetitions, covering a period of one week, were necessary to change the originally slightly unpleasant-feeling tone of this combination:

into a neutral tone for a seven-year-old child; two months of practice on a piano composition containing this progression:

changed it from an unpleasant stimulus to a decidedly pleasant one for a seventeen-year-old pupil.

How widely varying is the response of the individual to dissonance was shown when the following chord:

was played on the pianoforte. The four chosen
hearers expressed themselves as follows:

(1) 'Just a sound. It does not mean anything. Not
pretty, not ugly.' (2) 'Ugh! I hate it! Sounds all
wrong!' (3) 'Not specially nice. Could perhaps be
used better with other chords.' (4) 'I love it! It
reminds me of the 31st of December, when all the
whistles are blowing at midnight!' This last is an example of the sensorial-imaginal response.

Probably most musicians would agree with No. 3, for
there are few conglomerations of notes that cannot
be justified by their context.

It is inevitable that a book of this kind should contain much that is inconclusive. Frequently one sees
unsatisfactory methods in classification, and other
details that would have been avoided had competent
musical advice been sought. The competence appears
to be confined to the scientific side, the musical parts
of the book showing the hand of the dabbling amateur.
Nevertheless it is a welcome first step in a branch
of study that may some day yield valuable results.
And if the reader is moved to irreverent levity here
and there, he has only to follow the advice quoted
above, and subdue his hilarity by turning on a record
of the 'Pathetic' Symphony, or some other work calculated to lead to 'a decrease in function of the cardio-
vascular system'. He can find out when to stop the
Symphony by taking note of his pulse-rate and systolic
and diastolic blood-pressure, or by glancing at his
Tycos sphygmomanometer.

MUSIC AND TEARS

WRITING from Rome in 1639, the Abbé Maugars, describing Italian music, said that a certain performance so ravished him that he forgot his mortal condition, and felt himself to be already among the angels.

At about the same date our own Thomas Mace wrote:

We had for our Grave Musick, Fancies of 3, 4, 5, and 6 Parts to the Organ, Interpos'd (now and then) with some *Pavins, Allmaines, Solemn, and Sweet Delightful Ayres;* all which were (as it were) so many *Pathetical Stories, Rhetorical, and Sublime Discourses; Subtil, and Acute Argumentations; so Suitable and Agreeing to the Inward, Secret, and Intellectual Faculties of the Soul and Mind;* that to set them forth according to their *True Praise, there are no Words Sufficient in Language;* yet what I can best speak of Them, shall be only to say, *That They have been to myself, (and many others) as Divine Raptures, Powerfully Captivating all our unruly Faculties, and Affections, (for the Time) and disposing us to Solidity, Gravity, and a good Temper; making us capable of Heavenly, and Divine Influences.*

And in 1668, Pepys, writing in his Diary of a performance of *The Virgin Martyr,* says:

But that which did please me beyond anything in the whole world was the wind-music when the angel comes down, which is so sweet that it ravished me, and indeed, in a word, did wrap up my soul so that it made me really sick . . . so that neither then, nor all the evening going home, and at home, I was able to think of anything, but remained all night transported, so as I could not believe that ever any music hath that real command over the soul of a man as this did upon me.

There is no doubt as to the sincerity of these old records of the emotional effects of music; and there are many well authenticated instances of much later

212

date. We all know, for example, the delight Berlioz
felt when one of his works caused members of the
audience to faint. Tears must have been a common
feature of the concert-room in Beethoven's day, judging from contemporary reports; moreover, he said,
in one of his cynical moments, 'Pooh! 'tis not their
tears we musicians want, but their applause.' Yet he
himself wept as he wrote the Cavatina in the B flat
Quartet, and could never hear it afterwards without
being overcome. Much as we enjoy that beautiful
movement, I doubt if it has turned on the lachrymal
tap for many a long day. In fact, the recent temporary
decline in Beethoven's popularity was partly due to
this strongly emotional quality in his music. Emotion
being out of fashion—or, at all events, the kind of
emotion roused by fine music—the most frankly
emotional of composers must needs be under a cloud.

We are even less responsive to the macabre and
terrific. For this reason I believe the periodical attempts to create something like a Berlioz boom are
unlikely to succeed. Take away the 'fat boy' element
in Berlioz, and there is too little left to enable him to
compete with the really big all-round composers. No
doubt he made our forefathers'—and especially our
foremothers'—flesh creep, but his most horrific moments cannot now raise so much as a square inch of
goose-flesh. We are merely amused at his madness,
and interested in his method. At recent performances
of the 'Fantastic' Symphony, I found that the 'March
to the Scaffold' and the 'Witches' Sabbath' roused in
me, and in all my neighbours so far as I could see,
nothing more than a suppressed hilarity of the kind
we should feel if somebody read Mrs. Radclyffe to us.
I almost wrote Poe for Mrs. Radclyffe, but remembered that Poe at his best moments has still the authen-
tic touch of horror. In fact, the 'fat boy' in literature
and painting is much more lastingly successful than
in music.

§

In his *Studies in Modern Music*, Sir Henry Hadow says that Berlioz

. . . can inspire wonder but not awe, terror but not reverence, and much of the work which he intended to be most impressive resolves itself into a series of scenes which sometimes rise to the level of the Inferno, and oftener sink to that of the Musée Wiertz.

It is only fair to remember that this was written in 1892. I doubt if Sir Henry would still find Berlioz so terrible and wonderful; music depending largely on sensational elements is invariably the first to suffer from old age. Yet I imagine that, so far as horror is concerned, the mad painter can touch the spot more frequently and completely than the not quite sane composer. At all events, I have collected more nightmarish feelings in five minutes at the Musée Wiertz than from the whole of Berlioz.

This is no doubt a common experience. If so, it proves that music has not only ceased to be a lachrymatory stimulant; it has also lost its power to harrow.

There are two reasons for this. First, the war made such an assault on both our pity and terror that for a long time to come the provocative powers of any kind of art must be badly discounted. A man who has had a real tragedy in his life is apt to be unmoved by the imaginary sort, no matter how skilfully presented; and when a whole continent has had four years of accumulated tragedy, the inevitable result is a public that is indifferent to, or frankly contemptuous of, pre-war emotional stimuli. Not that we remain stony. On the contrary, we have exchanged the old emotion for hysteria, which is easily aroused by a variety of things that would formerly have left us calm. Thus, in 1926, during the closing stages of an international golf match, the defeat of a popular cham-

214

pion so profoundly affected the onlookers that many of them watered the green and filled the fatal final hole with their tears. It is true that the majority of these afflicted ones belonged to the race that under the hardest of exteriors carries the softest of hearts— the Scots; but even we comparatively reserved English are little better. We have lost the despised Victorian stolidity and solidity, religious outlook, and response to emotional music; instead we babble and slobber over a hundred things that don't matter; and we are too clever to be religious, but sufficiently foolish to be superstitious. (Soothsayers make a good living, and it is a common thing to find local authorities granting —without laughter—petitions that in the numbering of a street the unlucky 13 should be omitted!)

§

I said above that there were two reasons for the decline of the appeal of music on the emotional side. The more obvious one is the war, but perhaps the other is hardly less powerful. To old Thomas Mace and the Abbé Maugars music was a refreshing experience largely because it was new, and even more because they had so little of it. Moreover, the making and hearing of music was then an end in itself, whereas to-day we not only have far too much music, but an immense proportion of it is a mere humble constituent in another function. When even a first-rate orchestra plays at a restaurant, which matters most to the hearers—the music or the meal? Admitting the value of light music as a background to social and recreative occasions (it has to be remembered that we owe to this use of it many delightful things by Mozart and Haydn), I fancy most of us are beginning to feel that the art is suffering from being cheapened by its constant association with eating and dancing, and through playing a prominent part in many forms of entertainment of tenth-rate quality.

A close time for music of all sorts—or a year's abstinence from concerts—would do us and the art a power of good. Orpheus with his lute might then recover some of his old powers. At present he is so much of a standing dish that for the sake of his credit and our appetite he should go off the menu for a bit.

Yet there are probably few middle-aged folk who have not wept at music on occasion. Even music critics at the beginning of their career were of penetrable stuff.

Has anybody ever seen a critic beguiled of a tear during the execution of his duty? The question seems fantastic, but the answer is in the affirmative. I know, because I happen to have seen the prodigy —once. True, both time and circumstances were unusual. It was at one of the war concerts at Queen's Hall, during the performance of the finest bit of music inspired by the war in any country—Elgar's 'Carillon'. Next to me was ——, critic of the ——, and at the end, in the act of blowing my nose aggressively and unnecessarily, and turning my head in order to hide a shameful tear, I saw that my neighbour was in the same plight. 'Tis a dreadful thing to see a strong man weep, and the sight broke down defences already breached by the 'Carillon'. I may, perhaps, claim to be the only one who has ever seen a critic thus melt.

It would be interesting to put a questionnaire to half a dozen average readers, thus: (1) Have you ever been moved to tears by a piece of music? (2) If so, how many of such occasions can you easily remember? and (3) What was the music? I don't mind exposing myself in the interests of scientific inquiry, so I lead off by replying: (1) Yes; (2) Four; (3) The opening bars of the 'Meistersinger' Overture; a short passage in a Mozart chamber work, the identity of which I have forgotten; 'The Death of Minnehaha'; and the 'Carillon' aforesaid. With reference to (2), I ought in fairness to add that I do not count (I couldn't, because of their number) the occasions when I have been bowled over by the singing of a crowd, or by children's choirs at competitive festivals (a man must be toughly-bowelled if he is to hold up against the more appealing of these youngsters). But here the cause is largely non-musical. In fact, it will usually be found that even when we are moved by a piece of pure music (independent of any text or programme, that is) there will often be found some contributing cause.

Thus, I have heard the 'Meistersinger' Overture many hundreds of times, but only once has it affected me in this particular way; and on the solitary occasion there was a reason, though a curious one. (I set all these things down, at the risk of being called an egoist, because I think there is real interest, and even value, in analyses of our reactions to music. Perhaps it is Frank Howes's recently-issued book, *The Borderland of Music and Psychology*, has made me thus reckless in the pursuit of knowledge. Anyway, I believe Mr. Howes is right in saying that concert-givers, and performers generally, have thought too little about the psychology of their audiences.) As to that 'Meistersinger' Overture and the tear it drew: The occasion was an afternoon concert, and I had come almost direct from a City church, where I had writhed under some of the worst singing of Palestrina I had ever heard. It was still in my mind, and I was reflecting on it (not without bitterness), when the orchestra began the Overture. The contrast between its splendid opening phrase, delivered by a disciplined force, and the scratchy, out-of-tune outrage on Palestrina that I had heard an hour or two before, was overwhelming, and I succumbed at once.

I have heard of others being affected in similar circumstances, e.g. harassed teachers and choir-trainers coming straight from stumbling lessons to a concert-room. But I do not agree that a technically perfect performance needs to be contrasted with an indifferent one in order to affect us emotionally. The longer we live the more susceptible we become to the appeal of the technical side of composition—beauty of form, the easy mastery of some problem in construction, and so forth. And the same probably holds good in performance to a greater extent than we imagine. It is humbug to pretend (as many people do) that a technically flawless performance is necessarily cold. Some even seem to think that a goodish proportion of wrong notes is indicative of a poetic and musical temperament. But as there are plenty of bungling players and singers with the temperament of a codfish, it is clear that mere inaccuracy is an unreliable thermometer. Yet the attractiveness of a difficulty overcome with ease is such that if one of these codfish acquires technical mastery, his performance will be far from negligible. If he can play the notes fluently and correctly, with the modest amount of nuance and flexibility that may be expected from one so completely withdrawn from his native element, he will enable the composer to deliver his message sufficiently to move us, if there be any moving quality in it.

Of all popular solo instruments the pianoforte seems to move us least. Is this due to its fatal defect— lack of *sostenuto*? The violin can search our very heart-strings, the human voice can do so even more easily (thanks to the aid of words), the organ at times, a chorus very often: all these can give us sustained melody. The pianoforte can stimulate us, and is perhaps capable of a greater variety of amusing effects than any other instrument; but its inability to draw a long melodic line is against its doing more. There is irony in this, seeing that its repertory is rich in music bearing highly emotional labels.

The Mozart passage made its effect simply by its pure beauty as sound. It had no special emotional significance, nor was there any striking effect of rhythm or dynamics. It was just a sudden glimpse of sheer loveliness of part-writing and tone-colour. (I fancy it was one of the chamber works for string quartet and one wind instrument.)

As for the Coleridge-Taylor work: here of course the poignant text is so important a factor as almost to disqualify it for inclusion in my list. But we must give the composer credit for music that greatly heightens its appeal. In order to gauge the extent of his contribution you have only to ask yourself to what extent the poem alone would affect you if you merely read it before hearing the setting. As things are, even if you never hear the music again, you will never be able to read the poem unmoved. The passage I refer to specially is that beginning on p. 106 of the vocal score, 'Farewell, Minnehaha'; and I remember the occasion particularly well, because the first time I heard the work was at a rehearsal in which I was one of the choir. When this page came along I was only one of many who gave up singing. A few of my colleagues held on, but a large proportion of the singers found it necessary to adjust their glasses, or fumble with their copy, or cover up their sudden silence in some such way. (If I remember rightly, much the same thing happened at the first performance of the work—at Hanley, wasn't it?—the choir being so overcome as to break down temporarily.) The points that seem to emerge from this inquiry are: (1) The occasions on which one is moved to tears by a piece of music—especially a piece for instruments only, and free therefore from the added appeal of text and human voice—are few; (2) That even in those few cases it will be found that there is often some predisposing condition of the hearer, or other fortuitous element. And if you want proof of the failure of music, compared with literature or drama, as a provocative of tears, you have only to note that dozens will weep at a theatrical performance of (say)

Romeo and Juliet, whereas Tchaikovsky's orchestral work of the same title draws never so much as a sniff. (3) The emotional appeal is greater in concerted than in solo music, the combination of chorus and orchestra being specially potent. (Here there are two extra-musical factors: (*a*) the text, and (*b*) the effect of a large number of people doing something in common. Hence the fact noted by Berlioz—that a single soldier grounding his musket is insignificant, whereas a regiment doing it is overwhelming, both to eye and ear.) (4) The actual quality of the music is often a negligible point, especially in large-scale performances. (5) A passage may move us profoundly one day, and fail to touch us on another.

A further point is sufficiently curious to deserve a paragraph to itself. I don't know whether my experience is singular, but I have found that slow movements of the classical school, marked *patetico, appassionata, con gran espressione, dolente,* and the like, almost invariably fail to touch the spot however much they may delight *qua* music. Probably this is because fashion changes in emotional stimuli, as in other things, and what moves one generation may easily bore the next.

I suggest as a further reason that the actual slowness of the average slow movement is against it. Emotion of the moist and irrepressible sort is more often than not the result of a sudden appeal, or a touch of the unexpected. A leisurely and calculated affair may induce a pensive melancholy, but rarely does more. Few even do so much.

Hence the loss of appeal of such things as the Adagio of the ninth Symphony, which to many people to-day is infinitely less moving than the mysterious opening passage, certain passages in the Scherzo, the emergence of the theme of the Finale, and the two presentations of it immediately following, with their exquisite polyphony.

§

The conclusion of the whole matter is that we have
lost something the Abbé Maugars, Thomas Mace, and
Pepys possessed—the power of being rapt away easily
by music. With them, almost any concord of sweet
sounds was enough; with us, there must usually be
something to back up and accentuate the appeal of
the music—associations, a programme, a war, or what
not. Often a touch of liver is responsible, and then
the matter is physiological rather than psychological.

But what we have lost in one direction we appear
more than to have made up in another. The great
bulk of the finest music is something far better than
a mere stimulus to the more facile emotions. Not till
to-day, apparently, have rank-and-file music lovers
(hearers as well as performers) been able to appreciate
music whose appeal is largely—even primarily—to
the mind. Hence the great and growing public for
the organ and clavier works of Bach (especially the
'48'), and for classical instrumental music generally.
Kindred signs are the revival of old polyphonic choral
music, and the tendency of the best modern music to
develop along the lines of polyphony rather than of
harmonic experiment. Significant, too, is the rapid
growth of the public for chamber music.

'What do you mix your colours with?' somebody
asked a painter. 'With brains,' was the reply; and
the familiar anecdote may be applied to any composer
of standing. Reaction to the intellectual side of music
is a comparatively new thing, so far as the general
musical public is concerned, and it is the best of
portents, because it will bring into currency a great
deal of music that the more emotional hearers of the
last generation dismissed impatiently as 'dry'. It is
not by mere chance that this growth of appreciation
of the intellectual side of music coincides with the

decay and disappearance of the 'ballad concert', with
its facile appeal to the emotions. The pendulum may
swing that way again, but popular music of the future
will gain from the present reaction against the lachry-
mose. It will be better *qua* music, and it will reflect
life more faithfully, because popular creative artists
will realize that in the normal life thought plays at
least as big a part as emotion.

§

Now that the cinema manager has seen the possibilities of music as a tear-producer, mere musicians
must more than ever steel themselves to listen dry-
eyed. Among my newspaper cuttings is one headed:

'TEAR MUSIC FOR FILM STARS'

It tells us that 'the sensitive young people who act
for the pictures' now scientifically exploit the possibilities of music in this way. They declare themselves
unable to reach emotional peaks without the stimulus
of their pet 'passion tune'.

'Sadness from a Sonata' is the next caption, followed by:

Thus Wanda Hawley, the golden-locked U.S. star,
told me that the melody she invariably employs to
induce excessive sorrow is the *Kreutzer* Sonata.
Wherever she travels Wanda's indispensable tear music
accompanies her in the form of a gramophone record
and a tiny portable gramophone.

Leaders, Beethovenites especially, will be glad to
know how the golden-locked Wanda uses this
'melody':

The Ecstatic Shiver

At the Gaumont Studios, during the week, she gave
me ocular proof of her method. As she faced the
camera for a pathetic scene for *The Lights o' London*,
Beethoven's wailing notes murmured from the music

box. Drinking in the dolorous tones the little actress shivered ecstatically. A moment later pearl-like tears —indisputably genuine—welled in Wanda's eyes; the kinematographer softly turned the handle, and the touching scene was quickly completed.

A wasteful, laborious method: Mr. Vincent Crummles would have unsealed the fount more quickly than Wanda, and at a fraction of the cost.

He would have peeled an Onion.

A DEFENCE OF OPERA

Q.—Would you go so far as to say that grand opera is the keystone for the building of a musical nation? What about chamber music, symphonic music, instrumental music of all kinds?

A.—I feel strongly that we cannot become a really musical nation until we give first consideration to grand opera. I believe it is the most representative of all musical art forms because it takes on all of them for its successful expression.

WILLIAM S. BRADY, *in an interview in 'The Musician'.*

We may admit that English people do not support opera. But why should they be blackguarded for that? Operas, with very few exceptions, provide a prehistoric kind of entertainment, and the English failure to support them may be really a mark of civilization.—COMPTON MACKENZIE.

THE curious view of opera as the last word in music and the touchstone of taste, is not confined to Mr. William S. Brady and other enthusiasts across the water. We on this side have our Bradys, who periodically demand a subsidized opera, and point to our lack of enthusiasm for opera as a proof of musical inferiority to the Continent. Very well; if opera be the test of musical culture, we accept the challenge of the Bradys. The greatest opera-going public for generations has been that of Italy. What sort of figure does Italy cut in musical history since the great days of her polyphonic school?

The worst stage in the musical life of France was the period just before the renaissance brought about by Franck and a few others—a period when the public flocked to operas of a superficial type that (as Bruneau said) threatened to deal the death-blow to music.

From time to time the British public is scolded because it has no subsidized opera. 'Look at Ruritania,' say our mentors. 'Even so small a state as Ruritania, not much bigger than Rutland, manages to run a national opera. Look at such cities as Pum-

pernickel-am-Spree, at Amsterdam, at Rotterdam, at
Seidlitz, at— in short (the supply of names giving out)
simply look! If Pumpernickel can run its opera all
the year round, why cannot Cheadle? If Seidlitz, why
not Epsom? The answer is that all these Continental
people are musical, and we English are not. Opera
is the acid test, and our indifference to it proves that
we have no music in our souls, whatever else we may
have there.' And in similar strain we are given to
understand that concert-attendance is another test
from which we emerge as mere barbarians.

But I deny the validity of both tests. There was
abundance of musical life here and on the Continent
long before there were concerts or opera-houses.
Otherwise, the musical history of England begins with
the name of Thomas Britten. But we know that we
had quite a decent musical past to our credit long
before Thomas combined a coal round and a box-
office. And our musical life would not suddenly dry
up if all our concert-rooms and opera-houses were
promoted to cinemaship. Despite the Jeremiahs, there
are still many hundreds of thousands of us to whom
music is a part of life. We should continue to take in
our daily supplies via the gramophone, the player-
piano, and the wireless. Nor should we stop at that.
We should still lift up our voices in choral societies
(Sir Thomas Beecham, in an article written to prove
that we were musically bankrupt, once said that this
country had four thousand choral societies. I give his
total from memory, but I know it ran into thousands.
Anyway, that one sentence proved that so far from
being bankrupt we were by way of being a jolly sight
more solvent than the opera-eating Ruritanians. A few
thousand choral societies, in village, suburb, and city,
working at the madrigalists, Bach, Elgar, and our fine
modern English part-song composers, imbibe and
spread more musical culture than any number of
opera companies whose staple is early Verdi, Puccini,

Massenet, &c., with an occasional Wagner cycle or dash of Mozart); we should still continue our amateur chamber music and orchestra activities; our hundreds of competition festivals would go on dealing with their many thousands of entrants; the parlours of a million homes would still resound with our assorted instrumental solos and duets; and the voice of the family vocalist would still be heard in the land—or, at all events, by the people next door. Run over in your mind all the musical folk among your circle of relatives and friends, and you will find that a good proportion of the keenest and most musical rarely or never go to either concerts or opera. I do not deny that they miss something by this absention, but I deny also that they are necessarily less musical than the average concert- and opera-goer.

As for opera: you may claim much for it, at its best, as an attractive blend of arts, but (as we see) our attempt to use it as a gauge of a nation's musical standing is likely to lead to unexpected results.

§

Perhaps the most damaging charge to be brought against opera is that it calls for an expenditure out of proportion to the artistic result. I am well aware of the short-sighted folly of demanding that art shall 'pay' in the direct, hard cash sense of the term. The real profit that the community derives from any artistic or cultural enterprise is of the kind that cannot be appraised, so we must not look too closely at the bill. At the same time the bill cannot be ignored, and when it is so heavy as it is in the case of opera, we shall be foolish if we don't inspect it pretty closely, and ask ourselves if so costly a game is worth the candle.

Certainly opera is the very last form of enterprise for which a State subsidy can fairly be claimed. Not only does it yield a comparatively meagre artistic return for a vast outlay; there is the further objection

226

that whereas concerts, free libraries, public parks, playing fields, &c., benefit the major part of the population, opera can be enjoyed only by the minimum. There is hardly a small town, large village, or drab suburb, unable to benefit from some at least of the amenities provided by the rates, whereas opera can be given only in the large towns and cities where there is a theatre fit for the purpose, and a public large enough and sufficiently affluent to fill it. When this country once more finds itself with money to burn and has done all that can be done in the way of subsidizing orchestras, competitive festivals, touring chamber-music and other concert parties, &c., it will be justified in considering the subsidizing of opera, and not before.

Until that day the enthusiasts for opera—a *mélange* that takes half a dozen fine arts and usually spoils most of them—must be prepared to foot the bill themselves.

The indignant reader who protests against that last sentence must calm himself and face the facts. Out of all the many hundreds of operas, are there more than a mere handful that can be regarded seriously from the combined points of view of music, literature, drama, and scenic effect? Comparatively few will bear scrutiny on the score of music, and we can enjoy these as a rule only by closing our ears to the absurd libretto, shutting our eyes to the acting or scenery (or both), and switching our intelligence off from the plot. Apart from the pick of Wagner, I doubt if there are a dozen operas that a musician can whole-heartedly admire *so far as his art is concerned.* (This is a test that cannot be shirked by those who claim that opera is the greatest of musical forms.) One of those few exceptions is Verdi's *Falstaff*, and it is a damning fact that this masterpiece is one of the least performed of the composer's works. Would this be the case if operatic audiences were on the same level of musical intelli-

gence as those who attend orchestral and chamber
concerts? (I am not forgetting the practical difficulties
that are alleged to prevent frequent performances of
Falstaff. But so long as the opera public is content
with repetitions of a few inferior favourites, managers
are not likely to put themselves out over *Falstaff*.)

§

The fact is, opera is necessarily so hampered by
conventions, makeshifts, and compromises, that a
first-rate composer touches it at his peril. Wagner
comes out of the ordeal with flying colours, but even
he provides the best of evidence as to the weakness
of opera as a musical form. If opera were so successful
a blending of the arts as is claimed, how comes it that
so much of the music of Wagner's best operas can be
enjoyed in the concert-room? In whole stretches of
The Ring, *The Mastersingers*, *Tristan*, and *Parsifal*,
we can dispense not only with the scenery and action;
we can even replace the voice with an orchestral instrument, and listen to the result with more pleasure
than is given by many a purely orchestral work. The
explanation is that Wagner was not so much an opera
composer as a great symphonic writer who took the
wrong turning. The time may yet come when we
shall see that one of the greatest disasters in the history
of music was Wagner's stopping at his first Symphony.
What a group of symphonic masterpieces he might
have given us—not merely that tenth Symphony for
which the world was waiting. He would have gone
on and made the tale twenty.

Musicians who attend a Wagner opera go to hear
rather than to see. Many can enjoy *The Ring* only by
closing their eyes—in other words, by ignoring all the
constituents of opera save one. Give them the music,
and anybody may have the remainder—the long-
winded text and the clumsy paraphernalia. The Zoo,
the circus, and the cinema can supply most of these

things far better. Of all the standard operas there are few compounded of (1) music that will bear scrutiny *qua* music, (2) a text that is at least a sound piece of work on literary grounds, and (3) a story with human appeal and probability told with genuine imagination.

On the other hand, the most widely successful operas are usually the work of third-rate composers who have what is called 'a sense of the theatre'—which often means a knack of writing music just good enough to help out the dramatic situation, but not sufficiently good to distract attention from it. A similar lowering of standards prevails in other departments. Thus, it is a physical and psychical impossibility for the principals to give us simultaneously acting and singing of the very best. Also, the text must not be unduly witty or significant, because the exigences of vocalism will make it difficult or impossible to 'put across'. Even if it can be delivered convincingly the hearer is so busy watching the acting and listening to the music that he can spare very little attention for the text. So it follows that opera demands of its constituent arts that they shall be always an appreciable degree below their best, in order that they may not kill one another. Only in the Overture or Intermezzo may the composer let himself go—whereupon enthusiasts for this 'greatest of musical forms' usually drown his efforts with chatter. Is it surprising that with few exceptions the most popular operas have been written by composers who have done little or nothing worth hearing in the shape of pure music? This is another way of saying that they couldn't or wouldn't write music good enough to stand on its own feet and hold our interest unaided. On the whole I think 'couldn't' is the word. If you disagree, look down the list of opera composers in Kobbé's *Complete Opera Book*. They are all there—the merest handful of somebodies and a host of nobodies.

§

The literary and dramatic feebleness of the average opera is admitted on all hands, and is tolerated for the sake of the music, or of a few brilliant snippets. No other form of art is allowed to cumber the ground on such slender excuses as appear to be sufficient for the repeated performance of certain operas. At a recent Italian season at Covent Garden several works —e.g. *Fedora* and *Lucia di Lammermoor*—were put on merely to give a *prima donna* an opportunity for display. This is true to tradition, for Donizetti's *Elixir of Love* was revived at the Metropolitan, New York, in 1904, solely in order that Caruso might be heard in the romance in Act II, 'Una furtiva lagrima'. Nobody pretended that this early example of Donizetti contains anything else worth hearing. Yet a huge audience sat out a feeble work lasting a whole evening in order that a tenor might disport himself in one air!

Burning the pig-sty in order to roast the pig is an economical proceeding by the side of this. Imagine a parallel case in any other form of music, e.g. an orchestral concert of poor music, selected with a view to giving the conductor a five minutes' purple patch, or for the sake of a little bit of solo work by one of the players! It would never happen, simply because, with all their faults, concert-goers know pretty well what 's what in orchestral music. If it be objected that they allow virtuoso conductors to confine themselves mainly to hackneyed works, the answer is that usually the hackneyed works are at least fine music. Moreover, what is hackneyed to the critic and to the regular concert-goer is often novel to many in the audience. The C minor Symphony perhaps holds no more thrills for you and me, but to the man in the next pew it may be a revelation. What has the *Elixir of Love*, or *Fedora*, or *Lucia* to reveal to anybody?

Opera does harm to the cause of singing in a variety

of ways. One of the worst bits of singing I have ever heard was in *Pagliacci*, when the performance of the Prologue was marked by practically every vocal fault —wobble, bad intonation, *portamento ad nauseam*, and distorted rhythm. But the singer looked the part and certainly could act, so the doped and dazzled audience roared its approval of singing that would have been tolerated nowhere else. There must have been a good many young vocal students present: what sort of a lesson and example was it for them? Again, consider the gramophone records of operatic singing in which the tenors alternately yell and sob, the baritones blast and bellow, and the women mostly scream. It is no exaggeration to say that of every dozen of such records barely one is free from bad taste or bad vocalism, or both. What sort of a lesson is *that* for thousands of young singers?

§

But the crowning weakness of opera is that it leaves practically nothing to the imagination. To-day it is the fashion to sneer at oratorios and cantatas as Victorian and unimaginative. We are told that it is absurd for an oratorio soloist to personate (say) Elijah. 'Elijah', says the scoffer, 'didn't wear a boiled shirt, and didn't denounce the prophets of Baal to an orchestral accompaniment.' (Objections of this type might as reasonably be made to the singer of any kind of song demanding characterization, or to most elocutionary performances.) But which representation of *Elijah* calls for more imagination on the part of performers and audience : an oratorio, in which the text and music alone tell the story? or an opera, wherein the Prophet is given a flowing beard, sandals, and a kind of toga? If, instead of seeing in your mind's eye the prophets of Baal leaping on the altar and cutting themselves with knives, you demand that a group of 'supers' or chorus singers shall more or less nimbly

231

leap and pretend to carve themselves, your imagination must be in a bad way. Your place is in the cinema, where that particular kind of mental deficiency is provided for. Thus, when the heroine scornfully pulls the ring from her finger and throws it on the ground, you will be given a 'close-up' showing, first the ring on her finger (a finger the size of a well-nourished adult leg), then the pulling-off and throwing, and finally another 'close-up', wherein you will see the ring reach the ground and go bounding off like a child's hoop. (This sample of brainlessness was seen at a London cinema not long ago.)

We can listen with pleasure to much of the music of the *Flying Dutchman*, if we are allowed to imagine certain of the scenes. But when we see (as I saw once at a performance of this work) a score of stout mariners hauling laboriously at a rope that proved to have at the end of it nothing more substantial than a mere knot; or (as happened at a recent revival) two ships side by side, one in calm water, the other in rough, and with the wind blowing strongly two ways at once, we are not thrilled, but merely disrespectful.

Opera will continue to be the scorn of a very large proportion of musicians, and of such of the public as have not the cinema-mind, until it sheds its crude and childish realism and properties, gives us first-rate music, stories that are not ridiculous, and texts that are not stilted and sometimes even ungrammatical. All the signs point to the gradual decay of 'grand' opera—the type in which absurdities were thickest. Few, if any, more works will be written in that style. The Wagner music-dramas will continue to be given; we shall endure the *longueurs* and the comic properties for the sake of the music. But new works will be short, slighter in texture, and based on stories worth the telling.

The Beggar's Opera has shown us that the old ballad opera was not so foolish a form after all. Given good

232

dialogue and first-rate songs, it may yet have a new
lease of life. And I am inclined to think that Holst,
in his Falstaffian Interlude, has taken the first step
towards something like a new type—one in which
rapid prose speech will for the first time be a constituent. Its setting presents problems that were not
all solved in *At the Boar's Head*. Even when the problems are solved there will be a further wait while the
singers acquire a diction as quick, clear, and significant
as that of the patter-song artist at the music hall.
There will then be another halt while audiences become sufficiently alert to keep abreast of a text that
moves almost at speech-pace instead of being doled
out fatly at the rate of about twelve words per minute,
or repeated *ad nauseam*. This is not to say that all
new operas will be of the quick-fire order, but merely
that the future lies mainly with the racy rather than
the long-drawn 'grand' type.

'Grand opera' is not in our bones. As a nation we
are too conscious of its absurdities and incongruities.
Our real bent is shown in Gilbert and Sullivan, and
by our flocking to the revivals of *The Beggar's Opera*
and *Polly*. There is hope and significance in the fact
that our composers are now working on lines that
promise to be far more characteristic and suitable to
our needs than the imitations of foreign 'grand' opera
that were being produced a couple of decades ago.

The increasing success with which opera is now
(1928) being broadcast is a hopeful augury. Such
presentation will develop an imaginative type of
listener, and it will improve the repertory by focusing
attention on the musical and literary sides. Freedom
from stage conventions and necessities will almost
certainly stimulate writers and composers in new
directions; and the standard of performance will gain
from the fact that the principals will be engaged on
their qualifications as interpretative singers alone.
Their acting ability, stature, and facial characteristics

233

will not come into the question. On the stage we must
have Evas and Walthers that *look* the part. Wireless
performances of the future may give us the finest
Walther yet heard—and he may be a Quasimodo to
the eye. In a very real sense, and for the first time
in the history of opera, a proverb will become a working principle: 'Handsome is that handsome does.'

Finally, we are sometimes told that opera is a good
means of approach to pure music. 'Get the man in
the street into the opera-house, and he is half-way to
Queen's Hall,' said somebody recently. Only half-
way, though, and likely to stay there. The man who
makes his introduction to music through opera will
inevitably associate the art with all sorts of extraneous
things—stories, acting, appeal to the eye, &c., and will
be so accustomed to regarding music as a mere constituent, that the genuine article will come as a cold
douche. No; for one concert-goer made by opera,
there are a hundred made by gramophone and wireless. The opera-house is not the place for the neophyte, but for the seasoned musician. The neophyte,
imposed on by the glow and glitter, is easily persuaded
into believing that he is assisting at an important
artistic function, and so his taste is vitiated. The
musician knows better. For him the average opera is
merely a superior and very expensive kind of variety
entertainment, to be attended with some indulgence.
Generally speaking, if he wants the best drama and
the best music he goes to the theatre and concert-hall
and takes them both 'neat'.

PS.—The angry opera-lover who manages to get
to the end of this article may wonder at the title. It
seems to me that one of the most pressing needs of
opera is to be saved from the more doting of its
admirers, so I've tried to save it.

MUSICAL CRITICISM

MUSICAL criticism is by way of becoming a regular 'silly season' topic. Although it makes good 'copy', many of the arguments and discussions are bound to be futile, because personal taste inevitably plays so big a part that the *de gustibus* tag comes in. Moreover, most speakers confuse genuine musical criticism—that is, the critical appraisement of music old or new—with the reports of musical performances written and published within a few hours of their occurrence.

I suggest that any future discussions on musical criticism shall have 'terms of reference' laid down, and that writers shall be made to stick to them. Thus, one heading should deal with musical criticism of the type that is represented by some of the best books in musical literature, e.g. Newman's *Study of Wagner*, Dent's *Mozart and the Opera*, Parry's *John Sebastian Bach*, Pirro's *L'Esthétique de Jean Sébastien Bach*, &c. Another section would be concerned with the reviewing of new music—a type of criticism that is perhaps the most difficult of all, because the writer rarely has an opportunity of hearing the music he is judging. As a rule the most he can do is to run over it at a pianoforte, and we know that most of the music produced to-day—at all events, the music that calls for serious review—is of a type that demands more keyboard dexterity than the average musical journalist can spare time to acquire or keep up. In the case of chamber and orchestral music, a good deal of choral music, and the more difficult songs, he has to depend on his ability to hear the music mentally. With due respect to the gifted folk who expect us to believe that their favourite method of hearing music is through the eye, I maintain that the ear is the only reliable medium, even for fairly simple things. Beyond dispute, then, the reviewing of new music is one of the most important and difficult branches of musical journalism; it is also among the less lucrative kinds, owing to the fact that it calls for the expenditure of a great deal of time with a disproportionately small amount of 'copy' as a result. Yet the ethics and various difficulties of the work have not been discussed so far as I am aware. One of our musical debating societies might well devote a session to it. Here are a couple of questions with which to open the ball: (1) In view of the fact that the reviewer is writing about music that he has not heard, ought he to confine himself to such questions as degree of difficulty, length, general style, &c.? (2) Would it not be better to avoid all unfavourable criticism, and to select for review only such works as the reviewer feels he can praise without a qualm? In other words, should he not play for safety and content himself with giving a list of 'The Best of the Month'?

Perhaps I may be allowed to suggest answers:

(1) Reviews limited to matter that can be got from the title-page, plus a word as to the degree of difficulty, would have the double drawback of being poor 'copy', and of merely duplicating information that the publisher's advertisement or catalogue already gives in a handier form. The interest of a review lies almost entirely in the critical side, which in the hands of a good musician able to express himself clearly may be of considerable value to the student.

(2) A list of the 'best only' implies that works not mentioned are among the worst; it condemns by implication, and so is less satisfactory than a directly unfavourable review which gives a reason for the adverse opinion. Nor should the reader hastily assume that an unfavourable review necessarily has a bad effect on the sale of a work. A review of any kind is a better form of publicity than an advertisement, because a lot of people miss advertisements, whereas most of them read the reviews. Moreover, the points

that call forth the strictures of the reviewer are sometimes the very ones that commend a work to certain
of his readers. I remember once meeting a composer
a year or so after I had pitched into one of his works.
To my surprise and relief, he began by thanking me
for that unfavourable review. Before its appearance,
he said, the work had hung fire; a few weeks after, the
sales went up and the failure had become a success.
I was glad to find that I had done him no material
harm, and said so, though I did not pretend to regard
the popularity of his music as being other than disastrous so far as public taste was concerned. This case
may be unusual, but only a few instances of the kind
are needed to back up my point that composers would
be the losers if reviewers ignored works that struck
them as inferior. The average composer, questioned
on this point, would say, 'Praise if you can, blame if
you must, but for heaven's sake don't ignore me!'

Other questions in regard to reviewing will suggest
themselves as being worthy of consideration. It is
time this really important form of musical criticism
received some attention from our deliberative bodies.

§

As for the writer of concert notices, nobody loves
him; the poor fellow had the usual rough passage
during the debate at a recent British Music Society's
Congress. Dr. Eaglefield Hull even went so far as to
say that rather than ask the critics their opinion, he
would prefer to consult the programme-boy. Mr.
Scholes, in the *Observer*, neatly pointed out that the
critics are perfectly willing to accept this statement as
indicative of Dr. Hull's tastes and preferences—which
I am sure is the last thing the Doctor wants them to do.
He will learn from this that when on the platform a
mere Doctor of Music scintillates at his peril; better
leave such sweeping and startling dicta to Bernard
Shaw, who has the trick of it, and whom nobody

takes too seriously. G. B. S., joining in the debate, mixed up a lot of shrewd common sense with his fire-works. Among other things he said (speaking of his early days as music critic of the *World* forty years ago) that 'even stockbrokers used to read my article every week, not because they were keen on music perhaps, but because it was interesting in itself'. There, in a nutshell, is the rationale of the concert notice. People who assume a lofty attitude and pooh-pooh it as mere 'clever reporting' are really paying it the highest compliment. The ability to write a first-rate report, whether it be of a murder trial, a horse show, or a concert, is less common than appears to be the case. We read many columns of newspapers because of our interest in the subjects, not because of any skill in the reporting. Rarely do we come across anything arresting on the purely literary side. We wade through all those yards of print not because of the quality of the report, but in spite of it. When good reporting is valued as it ought to be, we shall find people praising a writer of concert notices by some such remarks as: '—— is more than a mere music critic; his concert notices are so good that one might even call him a first-class reporter.'

It is difficult to understand the complaint of some speakers at the B.M.S. Congress as to editors of the daily press regarding concert notices almost entirely from the news standpoint. Why shouldn't they? What is a newspaper for if not to give its readers an account of the previous day's happenings? The com-mon-sense way of looking at concerts is to put them among the recreations and amenities, with the drama and sport. Reports of new plays, cricket matches, boxing, tennis, &c., all give us news, and yet have room for criticism. The best of these reports reach a very high standard. *The Times* reports of such events as the lawn tennis championship, for example, are both news and literature—really engaging articles

from which the player-reader could learn much.
Neville Cardus's book, *Days in the Sun*, like his
articles on cricket, shows what can be done by a
'mere reporter' when dealing with the game of games.
(It is worth noting that Mr. Cardus is now—1928—
chief music critic as well as cricket reporter for the
Manchester Guardian.) Everybody agrees that music
needs more publicity. Can there be a better way of
getting it than by inducing the average newspaper
reader to take in concert reports with the other news?
If stockbrokers forty years ago read weekly what
Bernard Shaw had to say about music, mainly because
they knew Shaw's articles to be 'good stuff', why
shouldn't their stockbroking sons be reading concert
notices to-day? Perhaps they are: there are plenty
worth their attention. The best of them are models,
throwing to the surface the important points in the
programme or the performance, and rarely without
the felicitous touch that keeps one reading. The
musician who can learn nothing from such 'reporting'
as this is past instruction.

§

A writer in the *Musical Courier* recently went too
far in pressing the news side. He said that the public
cares nothing about

. . . the art of interpretation, nor opera-giving, nor
anything else concerning art. What the public wants
. . . is informative, non-technical news.

He complained that concert notices

. . . give no idea of an artist's personality, of the
character of his offering or the quality of his reception,

and ending by declaring that

. . . it is time the critics discovered the public, and it
is time we were relieved of the flood of technicalities
that comes day by day from the press, and can only
interest professionals.

239

By a happy chance this same issue of the *Courier* contained a full-page advertisement of William Backhaus, in which were displayed reports of one of his recitals, by half a dozen of New York's best-known critics. Very readable notices they are, too, with no 'flood of technicalities', though only one seems to come near to the standard required by the *Courier* writer quoted above—that by Deems Taylor, which opens thus:

When Mr. Backhaus, playing his last recital of the season at Æolian Hall last night, paused after the second movement of the Beethoven Op. 108 Sonata, his hearers, instead of breaking into applause, waited in silence for the next movement to begin. Which is a striking comment, both upon Mr. Backhaus's playing and the sort of audience he draws. He is essentially a musician's pianist. He has no mannerisms nor platform tricks. He keeps his hands on the keyboard and his mind on the music. He does not make faces nor crack small jokes with the audience. He falls into no sculpturesque poses. Some of his hair is long, but more of it is missing, and the present scribe, for whom he has been mistaken upon occasion, is one of the few persons, probably, who is strikingly impressed by his personal beauty.

Here we have 'an idea of the artist's personality' and 'the quality of his reception'; and the reference to the player's hair (both present and absent) comes under the head of 'informative non-technical news'.

A generation ago much importance was attached to such matters as the size of the audience and the 'quality of the artist's reception'. Turning over the 1836 volume of the *Musical World* recently I found some concert notices in which this kind of information is entirely squeezed out the musical side. Here, for example, is the report of 'Mr. Mori's concert':

The Great Room in the King's Theatre being totally inadequate to the accommodation of the subscribers to the Annual Concert of this public favourite, the per-

formance was transferred to the Opera House itself.
The result was, that so large an audience assembled
as to fill the theatre. We did not perceive a box un-
occupied; while the pit and gallery appeared to be
crowded. The Italians, and the best of the English
singers were engaged; and the concert, which was a
choice one, extended to a very late hour. It has been
conjectured that Mr. Mori cleared £800 by this benefit.

Which was good business for Mr. Mori; but what he,
or 'the Italians, and the best of the English singers'
sang, or how they sang it, appears to have been of no
importance. Most of the concert reports of the period
contain a reference to the size and type of the audience
—'the room was respectably filled'; 'the company
appeared to be much gratified by the general performance'; 'the concert was numerously and fashionably
attended'; 'the room was crowded with high fashion',
and so on. But let it be added that many of these
Musical World notices are surprisingly good to read,
with their strong common sense and frank style.

§

The most unreasonable attack lately launched
against the musical critic came from a novelist—Mr.
Stacy Aumonier. He began by describing as 'a profound mystery' the fact that 'the artist is the only
member of the community who is allowed to be
libelled, bullied, or insulted, without redress or the
right to hit back'.

If [he went on] I wrote: 'I went yesterday into
Messrs. Booster's stores in Oxford Street, and saw a
dud line of blankets. I never saw such flimsy stuff.
And the price they are asking for them is wicked,'
Messrs. Booster would immediately put the law on my
track. I should be heavily fined, if not put in prison,
for making statements liable to damage their business.
But if I wrote: 'I went yesterday into the Queen's Hall,
and heard Mr. Skrape play the Saint-Saëns Concerto.

I never heard a worse performance. His tone is appalling, and his technique utterly inadequate,' people would say, 'Bright boy! that 's the stuff to give 'em!' Mr. Skrape would have no redress, and he could not answer back. And yet I should be damaging his business just as seriously as if I had made the statement in question concerning Messrs. Booster.

This seems sound enough until one begins to look into it. The analogy then begins to give at the knees, and soon collapses entirely. To begin with, Messrs. Booster are not in the habit of asking the critic to come and see their stock in order that he may publish his opinion on it; whereas Mr. Skrape not only invites the critics, but is mightily offended if they don't come. Moreover, the quality and price of blankets are matters of fact that can be demonstrated beyond question; but who can prove that Mr. Skrape's performance of a given work was *not* the worst the critic had ever heard? And tone and technique are matters of opinion as much as of fact. Mr. Aumonier's case would have been better had he written a typical concert notice instead of a parody. I can think of no music critics likely to write of Mr. Skrape as Mr. Aumonier's imaginary critic writes. Even if they felt that way about Mr. Skrape they would let him down with reasonable lightness. Mr. Newman, for example, might say in effect exactly what Mr. Aumonier's burlesque critic says, but without the crudity which makes the notice offensive.

By the way, I find myself wondering if Mr. Aumonier has read many of Mr. Newman's concert notices. He says:

Criticism in itself is useful, natural, and frequently stimulating, but in the present form in which it is served out in the Press it has a deceptive value to the reader, and an unfair hold over the performer. A critic like Mr. Ernest Newman talks about himself in a human, lovable way. He says things like this: 'I arrived rather late, and was sitting in a bad part of the hall, but my impression was,' &c. This is the right and candid way to criticize. We know not only whom, but the kind of man we are dealing with.

I have read E. N. for a good many years, and hope to read him for lots more, but I am bound to say I do not recognize him in that diffident 'my impression was'! If Mr. Aumonier really thinks this is 'the right and candid way to criticize' he should have adopted it when he set out to criticize the critics, and to accuse them of 'libelling, bullying, and insulting' the artist. 'I have not read the newspapers lately [thus he should have timidly ventured to remark] and my memory for such things is failing, so I cannot be sure; but I find it impossible to avoid an impression that critics are at times disposed to speak of artists with a degree of candour that is—well, not quate nace.'

And when Mr. Aumonier says that artists are 'libelled, &c., without redress or the right to hit back,' he is talking manifest nonsense. An artist has the same redress as other citizens. And as for 'hitting back', some of them spend a good part of their working life doing it.

Only in one point is Mr. Aumonier's article well-founded. He has us with him when he contends that all criticism should be signed. Criticism is the most personal of writing, and derives much of its interest from that fact. I look out each week to see what certain leading critics say of a work or a performance, not because I need their assistance in making up my mind, but merely because I want to see how they've made up theirs. And while I am finding out, I am pretty sure to get some fresh light on the work or the performance: even if, for once in a way, the little bit of extra light is thrown only on the critics themselves, I still have good value.

243

§

Far too much is made of the divergent views expressed by critics. Seeing that nobody expects them to agree in other matters where taste is a factor, why should we be aggrieved if they are not always in accord over music? And if one says 'white' and the other 'black', it only encourages me to go on holding stiffly to my preference for blue. Here, for example, are some findings, pilloried in the issue of *Musical Courier* from which I have already quoted. The *Mail* complained of a violinist—Josef Borisoff—that he 'relied too much on full vibrant tone, and too little on refinement . . . and [in the Franck Sonata] showed an inclination to tear emotion to tatters'. The *Herald* felt this, too: 'There was plenty of fire . . . perhaps more vibrancy and temperament and less refinement in Franck's Sonata than the Belgian composer would have enjoyed.' By this time you have a picture of Josef letting himself go, and putting the Franck across like a real he-man.

And now see Borisoff as he struck the *Sun*, the *Evening World*, and *The Tribune*: 'The strange weakness lurking in this excellent equipment was a certain coldness almost approaching routine.' 'One wishes that his tone were not so dry, and that he might put greater warmth into his playing.' 'The Franck Sonata . . . seemed calm and correct rather than expressive.'

You say that these extracts show the absurd inconclusiveness of criticism. I don't agree. One learns from them: (1) That Borisoff is an excellent fiddler; (2) that critics A and B differ from their brothers C, D, and E, as to the emotional content of the Sonata; and (3) that the player differs from both groups, being too warm for one, too cold for the other, and therefore almost certain to be right. If Borisoff is wise, he reads these notices with interest, refuses to regard himself as bullied, insulted, or libelled, and

244

continues to play the Franck as he feels it, and not as he gathers certain critics think he ought to feel it.

But how if such differences of opinion concern, not an interpretative, but a technical point? Then Borisoff, still wise, will begin by assuming that the adverse criticism is right, and will overhaul that part of his technical equipment, or take pedagogic advice, until he is satisfied that the criticism is wrong. In most cases he will find it is right, for the reason that critics rarely commit themselves to definite statements on technical points (especially in the direction of finding fault) unless they are well qualified and sure of their ground.

The lack of unanimity over which so much fuss is made is on the whole a good thing. A virtue or defect may easily escape one critic; it can hardly get past the whole gang. Anyway, good thing or bad, it is inevitable. *Quot homines* . . . Even Dr. Hull's panel of programme-boys would not always speak with one voice.

§

Among recent attacks on musical critics was one in a musical paper from a correspondent signing himself 'Anti-Humbug'. His main argument is as old as the hills:

Can the critics sing, play, conduct, or compose better than those they criticize? If not, their criticism is mere pretentious humbug to make a living—a casting the mote out of another's eye before they cast the beam from their own.

If we adopted this principle we should lose our right to complain in a hundred instances that occur in everyday life. When 'Anti-Humbug' finds his tailor spoiling the cut of a coat, or his cook sending up an uneatable dish, does he maintain an indulgent silence on the ground that he could not do better himself? He does not. And if the culprit turned on him with

245

the argument quoted above, he would reply that it was not his job, but the tailor's or cook's. Similarly the critic's business is not to sing, play, conduct, or compose (though there have been, and are, critics able to make a good show at one or more of these accomplishments); his office is to produce a readable judgement on the performance of others. And just as 'Anti-Humbug' is (presumably) a sound judge of a dinner, and able to point out the defects of one that falls short of perfection though (again presumably) but a poor cook himself, so any reasonably well-educated all-round musician can (after due preparation) be trusted to appraise the merits of a performance.

The position is summed up in an anecdote so well worn that I hesitate to repeat it: One of our best-known critics, judging some brass performances at a competitive festival, gave a decision unpalatable to a section of the audience. Came a Voice: 'What do *you* know about it? Can *you* play a brass instrument?' 'No,' replied the critic; 'nor can I lay an egg. But I know the difference between a good one and a bad one.'

The analogy is not perfect, of course, because the faults in an egg are not, I believe, connected with the laying thereof. All eggs are good when laid; the decline comes later. Still, the figure is near enough, and it has a homely smack that helps it with the crowd, as many a festival judge has found when dealing with classes that seemed to call for technical knowledge of a type that he did not possess. If everybody thought as 'Anti-Humbug' thinks, there would be an end to competition festivals, to reviewing of new books and music, and to examinations of all kinds. It is a notorious fact that some of the best musical examiners are men who through pressure of work, or the passage of years, are unable to keep their technique up to the mark. They must inevitably turn

down many aspirants whose actual technical skill is
superior to their own. Yet the longer they go on
examining, and the worse their own performing
powers become, the more unerringly can they lay
their finger on the weak spots of the examinees. For
the ability to size up a performance is largely a matter
of training, and a musical critic who year after year
listens with a keen and experienced ear (though with
an air of boredom and eyes deceptively closed) can be
relied on to give a good estimate of a performance.
Ask anybody who has tried his hand at this sort of
thing what he felt like at his first attempt. Hitherto
he had been merely listening like the rest of the
audience, ready enough to discuss the performance
orally; faced with the responsibility of committing
himself to a judgement on paper that will be read by
thousands next day, he has felt a good deal less light-
hearted about the task. For one thing, he found that
judging a picture or a book is easy in comparison,
because he could look at the picture again and again,
or go over bits of the book as often as he liked. Even
a play is fairly easy game, because it is a long, slow-
moving affair compared with a musical performance;
moreover, many plays are published as well as acted.
But a musical performance unrolls itself (often very
swiftly), and there is no turning back to revise your
impressions. (All this is painfully obvious, of course,
but the Anti-Humbugs have to be reminded of it.)
And when the critic has done this bit of skilled listening he has to use skill of another sort in putting his
hardly-won impressions on paper in a small space and
in a manner that shall be clear and attractive to the
average reader. Seeing how well our critics as a body
perform this double task of listening and writing I
think they receive a good deal less than their due.
'Anti-Humbug' criticizes the critics: they may well
turn his own feeble arguments on him, and ask him
if he could do better himself. Anyway, he may be

reminded that musical criticism has been a recognized craft for some generations now, and it will continue because it provides something demanded by the musical public, and, above all, by those who have something to criticize, whether as performers or composers. Those who have no use for it can easily avoid it.

'Anti-Humbug' ends by quoting the Russian parable of the donkey that tried, by braying, to show the nightingale how to sing. A good critic does this sort of thing much better. He shows people how to perform by pointing out merits and defects in such a way that the criticized, given gumption and a teachable nature, can learn a lot. If he tried to show them by actual performance he would be less convincing— probably even ridiculous. So he wisely sticks to his last, whereas the donkey, by lifting up his untunable voice in competition with the nightingale, gave himself away with both hooves, thus showing that he was not merely an ass, but a silly ass.